GREATER EXPECTATIONS

GREATER EXPECTATIONS

TEACHING ACADEMIC LITERACY TO UNDERREPRESENTED STUDENTS

ROBIN TURNER

STENHOUSE PUBLISHERS

PORTLAND, MAINE

Stenhouse Publishers

www.stenhouse.com

Library of Congress Cataloging-in-Publication Data

Turner, Robin, 1964-
Greater expectations : teaching academic literacy to underrepresented students / Robin Turner.
    p. cm.
Includes bibliographical references and index.
ISBN 978-1-57110-740-4 (alk. paper)
1. Minorities--Education (Secondary)--California. 2. Language arts (Secondary)--California. 3. Puente Project. 4. Hispanic Americans--Education (Secondary)--California. I. Title.
LC3726.T87 2008
373.1829009794--dc22
                    2007049721

Cover design and interior design by Blue Design (www.bluedes.com)

Cover photo by Kelly Johlic

Manufactured in the United States of America on acid-free, recycled paper

14 13 12 11 10 09 08 9 8 7 6 5 4 3 2 1

For Ron Archer, my high school English teacher, for providing me with the finest example of how to care for students, make teens feel like they matter, and never lose sight of the great wealth of humanity that is in every class, waiting to be developed.

CONTENTS

ACKNOWLEDGMENTS

No teacher succeeds alone. I am blessed to be surrounded by many good people who have supported me and sharpened my craft as a teacher.

My children, Kayley and Jared, have brought so much to my life over the last thirteen years. Thank you for being the best kids a dad could ever hope for. Kayley, you are, and will always be, the apple of my eye. Jared, you amaze me with your quiet interest in just about everything in life. I am immeasurably proud of both of you and thankful for the changes in my life that you have both brought.

April, thank you for the constant support you have shown me over the years. You've kept me grounded when I needed it and allowed me to fly when I had to. Thank you.

Jeff and Sandy Fitzpatrick have been loyal and true friends, and I wish I had more people in my life like them. You two mean the world to me.

Larry and Dianna Turner, Stan and Gail Savitski, and Bill and Karen Kelly have all played a part in my development as a father. Thank you.

Several teachers have made incalculable contributions to my life and career. I am eternally thankful to Joe Calwell for his mentoring during my first years of teaching. Joe, you taught me the importance of getting kids to *think*. I am also grateful to Richard Clarke, Dave Sturrock, and Sam Young for the camaraderie they allowed me to be a part of. They will always represent for me what teaching ought to be. Also, I am overwhelmed with appreciation for Rose Carroll and Tina Grossman, the original heroes of Mama Cozza's. Rose, for your loyalty and for always fighting for the kids, you are the female Atticus of Magnolia High School. We miss you. And finally, thank you to Linda Esping, who taught me nearly two decades ago that deep down, every kid wants to do well academically, and we just need to figure out a way to allow that to happen. I've yet to hear better teaching advice.

My mathematical *muchacha*, Kelly Johlic, has my everlasting admiration and respect for the teaching she does and the impact she has on the students. Thank you for constantly challenging me to do my very best at my job and for never letting me forget the incredible importance of the job we do.

My Puente *compadre*, Steve Gonzales, has also had a great influence on my life. My belief that he is the finest counselor in the state is unshakable. Thank you, Steve, for the impact you have had on literally thousands of students throughout your career.

The English department at Magnolia High School has been my second family for many years now. Although we have diverse personalities, we are bound together in our unbreakable desire to do what is best for our students. Michelle Waxman, Dana White, Sheri Krumins, Virginia Kim, Margaret Tagler, Esther Noh, Melissa Hunnicutt, Amie Howell, Katrina Mundy, Sarah Valenzuela, Lindsay Ruben, Cecilia Gonzales, and Kelly Gallagher, you surround me with dedication and competence (plus, you are all good-looking and funny). Katrina, thanks for the frequent Starbucks; know that your C.O. is proud of you. Michelle, your words of solace helped me through some difficult times and your friendship means much to me. Kelly, thank you so much for your constant guidance and helping me figure my way out of the jams. I can never repay all that you've done for me; I wouldn't be half the teacher I am without you.

My principal, Dr. Ken Fox, and his administrative team of Ron Milner, Eva Valencia, and Monique Krause have been very supportive of me even when I've been a trifle difficult. Thank you.

Likewise, Mike Matsuda, coordinator of Beginning Teacher Support and Induction (BTSA) at our district office, has inspired me with the competence and caring he displays for all students, especially those that might otherwise fall through the cracks. Mike, you are an unsung hero.

Words cannot convey the affection I hold for my family at the Puente Project: Frank Garcia, Josefina Canchola, Claudia Canizales, Lauren Klaffkey, Katherine Martinez, Kelly Soderberg, and all the Puentistas in California. You've taught me to believe the statement *sí, se puede*. I'm especially grateful to the following Puente teachers: Julie Lecense-Switzer, Ellen Laffler, Sharon King, Isaac Sanchez, Lizzette Olivares, Krista Rogers, Kristen Land, John Raya, Bettina Lopez, and Marcus Woodworth. A special thank-you to Dr. Jose Moreno, who can never be repaid for all that he has done for the program. Dr. Moreno, your passion for people is infectious.

The heart and soul of Puente, Jane Pieri, has stood in the gap and held the program together when it appeared cut from our state budget. Your tenacity in benefitting underrepresented students in California has changed thousands of lives. Personally, my career has been transformed because of your influence and belief in me. The respect I hold for you is immeasurable.

I am grateful for my American studies professors at Cal State Fullerton, Dr. John Ibson and Dr. Pamela Steinle, for teaching me the power and the value of culture.

I wrote this book while listening to countless hours of Bruce Springsteen, who often sings about those left behind, and I appreciate his commitment to the common man. He is the John Steinbeck of popular music.

For Nick and Jaden Baque, I wish you all the happiness in the world: 5 x ∞.

The group at Stenhouse Publishers have been wonderful to work with. Bill Varner, I cannot thank you enough for all the assistance, guidance, and encouragement you've shown me throughout the writing of this book.

Students like Renattha Contreras, Mike Crawford, Brenda Barajas, and Lauren vanderHorst have inspired me to do the best job possible. They embody everything that is good about students.

Finally, I need to thank the Puente class of 2010, who will always hold a special place in my heart. I was lucky to have been your teacher. Remember me when you write your book on salt.

CHAPTER ONE

Why Focus on Underrepresented Students?

IT WAS 1985, AND STUMBLING OUT OF BED, DISHEVELED AND GROGGY FROM THE RAVAGES OF THE CAREFREE NIGHT BEFORE AND ITS EFFECTS ON MY TWENTY-YEAR-OLD BODY, I ANSWERED THE DOOR, SQUINTING AGAINST THE BRIGHT LIGHT OUTSIDE. STANDING THERE WAS MY BEST FRIEND, MARK. WE WERE THREE YEARS OUT OF HIGH SCHOOL AND BOTH OF US HAD COMPLETED OUR LOWER DIVISION WORK AT A COMMUNITY COLLEGE THAT MAY. TODAY MARK WAS SUPPOSED TO START CLASSES AT CAL STATE FULLERTON; I, HOWEVER, HAD NOT EVEN GOTTEN AROUND TO REGISTERING FOR A SINGLE COURSE.

Mark told me that I *had* to register, and after I got cleaned up, he drove me to CSU at Fullerton and walked me to the admissions office. I paid the fee, which in 1985 wasn't nearly what it is today, and then he walked me to the last-minute registration area. Within a few hours, I was enrolled and registered for classes, and that night, I walked into my very first university classroom.

My life changed that day. My college education has enabled me to work at a job I love, earn a stable living, and more important, to better understand the complexities of life and possess the tools to solve the challenges that have come my way. That day was a significant turning point in my entire life, and it would not have happened had Mark not taken time out of his schedule to physically take me through the steps necessary for me to achieve my dream of a college education.

Such a small thing, really, not knowing how to apply for admission or how to register, and yet it very nearly kept me from getting my college degree. Coming from a family in which not one aunt, uncle, parent, or grandparent had ever attended a day of college, and no cousin had graduated high school, I was lucky to find guidance and direction from my friends regarding college; looking back, statistics show that for a kid like me, the chances of graduating from college were slim. Yet today my students overcome much greater obstacles than I ever did; my story pales greatly in comparison to the challenges placed before students of color in a working-class neighborhood today. I've never forgotten the day I was given assistance getting into college, and as a teacher, it still fuels me to work passionately toward enabling students to achieve their own goals.

When I first began teaching remedial English, I saw that my struggling students had dreams as well: some wanted to be able to get good jobs after high school, some wanted just to graduate, others wanted to go on to college. However, few of them really knew how to overcome the obstacles in their way, obstacles such as poverty, poor reading and writing skills, peer pressure on teenagers to not succeed in school, and an unfamiliarity with how to do well academically. Unfortunately, these obstacles often included the school system itself, which subtly pressured such students to substitute their dreams with much less lofty goals. The low expectations of school personnel, deficit-based school policies, and pedagogy that failed to address the background of non-white students often combined to create an insurmountable challenge for these students.

For instance, the counselors at registration treated some students differently from others. Students who "looked" collegiate had easy access to honors classes and college outreach programs like EAOP (Early Academic Outreach Program); students who wore baggy pants and oversized shirts were encouraged by counselors to take the easiest possible classes and were steered toward career programs such as Regional Occupational Program (ROP). Too often, the difference in treatment seemed to be based on ethnicity. Whites and Asians were treated with favor; Latinos and African Americans were assumed to be "at risk." To make matters worse, too many of my colleagues viewed the lack of success of African American and Latino students as a reflection of some cultural shortcoming rather than a problem inherent in the educational system or the individual educator. As a result, I witnessed too many students who remained poorly prepared for the future.

Veronica, a Latina freshman, was one such student. She was docile and quietly went along with her placement in remedial English and other lower-level classes, even though these classes did not fit in with her plans for college. She worked hard and was a good reader, but she struggled with writing; as a teacher, I was too young and inexperienced to really question why she was in my class. Both she and her mother treated educators with great respect and were reluctant to challenge the system. To be honest, I didn't provide her with as much academic rigor as a future college student would need. Although she did end up attending a community college and eventually got her B.A., she struggled greatly with the skills deficit that my school and I left her with.

Veronica belonged to a growing community of students, usually either African American or Latino, whose ethnicities were underrepresented at the university level. At the time, I began to notice the division at my school between the honors students—mostly white and Asian—and the students enrolled in my at-risk English class, nearly all of whom were Latino or African American. These students knew where they wanted to go, but didn't know how to get there.

I was only a few years into teaching, but I had stumbled onto a mission: to keep one eye on the future of my students, and find every resource possible that would help bridge the gap between where they were and where they wanted to be. I passionately wished to see the underrepresented students enrolled in my classes receive similar backing, but I wasn't quite sure how to pull it all together.

And then Puente came along. Founded in 1981 at Chabot Community College in Hayward, California, the program was expanded to the high school level in 1992; it currently directly serves over 43,000 students in California. The program bears some similarities to college-preparatory programs like Advancement Via Individual Determination (AVID), a national college preparation program aimed at students "in the middle" with GPAs of 2.5 to 3.5. The Puente program's mission is "to increase the number of educationally disadvantaged students who enroll in four-year colleges and universities, earn degrees, and return to the community as leaders and mentors of future generations" (Puente Project 1). Underrepresented students are placed together in the same Puente English class for two years and then are dispersed into Advanced Placement and college prep classes for their junior and senior years; a Puente counselor monitors them closely through all four years of high school. In a nutshell, Puente, the Spanish word for "bridge," provides accelerated reading and writing instruction, intensive counseling, and mentoring. As a result, "Puente high school students enroll at four-year colleges and universities at twice the rate of matched controls" (Puente Project 2).

Several years later, Veronica's younger sister, Sandra, enrolled in the Puente program. Like her sister, she was a sweet kid who stayed out of trouble and did well academically. This time, however, she was in a program that worked in her favor rather than working against her, valued her cultural capital, allowed her to read and study Latino literature alongside the classics written in English, and treated her ethnic background as an asset rather than a disadvantage. Because of two years of excellent instruction in reading and writing, and powerful guidance from the Puente counselor, Sandra was accepted to UCLA. Puente made it possible for Sandra to achieve her dreams of college; this same story is common to many families at my school.

Today I am two days into the school year. I have just been introduced to my new Puente English class—the ninth graders are excited but nervous, anxious but already feeling at home. One kid in particular, Johnny, has already caught my attention. You know that mischievous nervous energy that kids get when they are really enjoying a lesson? Johnny wears that look from the moment the bell rings until class is over. Today, his expression changed as we looked at the chart in Figure 1.1 that depicts the college-going rates of various ethnicities.

Figure 1.1 College-Going Rates of Recent Public High School Graduates by Racial-Ethnic Group, Fall 1990 and Fall 2003

	California State University				University of California			
	1990		2003		1990		2003	
	Number	Entry Rate	Number	Entry Rate	Number	Entry Rate	Number	Entry Rate
Asian	5,520	16.8	6,300	13.0	5,020	15.3	9,580	19.8
African-American	1,660	9.6	2,160	9.0	690	4.0	820	3.4
Latino	3,930	7.2	8,030	7.0	2,050	3.7	3,720	3.3
White	10,230	8.0	12,180	8.5	7,110	5.5	8,150	5.7

*Entry rate = number of entering freshmen from California public high schools as a percentage of the total number of graduates of California public high schools in that year.
(California Postsecondary Education Commission)

It was almost heartbreaking to see Johnny and his classmates tear apart the information here: only 3.3 percent of Latinos graduate from high school and go on to attend a UC school. Johnny admitted being "embarrassed by the numbers," and I could see his mischievous energy dim a bit. There's no way to sugarcoat this—our nation is doing a poor job of getting underrepresented students to the finish line, and that failure is going to have dire consequences for our society when those students graduate and enter the workforce. Johnny's eyes widened, his jaw dropped, and his head fell back as he absorbed the reality that if his classmates were to succeed, they would be defying the odds. At that moment, Johnny, the fourteen-year-old, one-hundred-pound freshman, had discovered that he had a passion to work toward improving the odds of success for underrepresented students.

Unfortunately, too many of our underrepresented students lack the assistance they need to cross the bridge from high school to university, and as a result, our workforce will surely suffer. From 1970 to 2000, the combined

5

population of underrepresented students exploded, increasing from 43 million to 72 million. This population grew at nearly double the rate of the general population (U.S. Census Bureau, Population Estimates). By 2025, one in four people of high school age in the United States will be Hispanic/Latino, but unfortunately, too many decision-makers in education are ignoring how quickly our nation is changing. Consider the charts in Figure 1.2a and 1.2b, taken from the U.S. Census. Figure 1.2a shows the rate of increase in the population of Latinos in the United States; Figure 1.2b shows the density of the Latino population in the United States.

Figure 1.2a

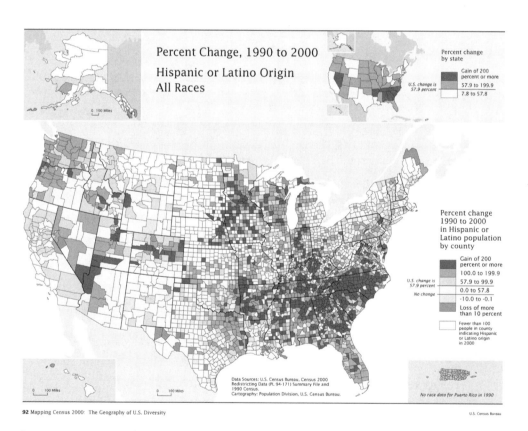

92 Mapping Census 2000: The Geography of U.S. Diversity   U.S. Census Bureau

(U.S. Census Bureau 2000a)

Figure 1.2b

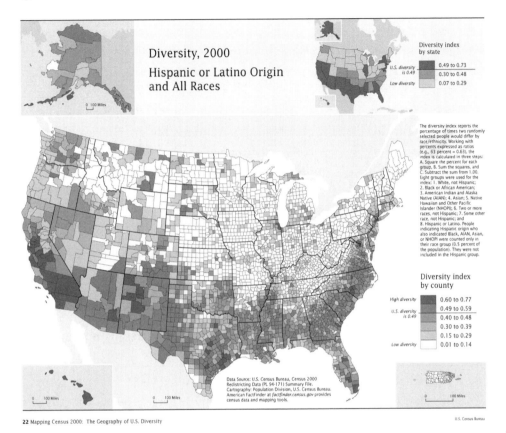

(U.S. Census Bureau 2000b)

These two charts reveal that almost every community in the United States either has a large Latino population or is experiencing a substantial increase of Latinos, which highlights just how important it is to close the educational gap. Over the course of the next fifty years, the total population that is white will have shrunk by more than 10 percent, while the Hispanic population will *double* (U.S. Census Bureau 2004). When you add the numbers of other underrepresented students, it becomes clear that we as a nation can no longer ignore the staggering failures of our educational system; we have to turn these numbers around.

Also, Latinos are four times as likely to drop out of high school as white students (U.S. Senate 2002). Even more troubling, while 33 percent of white students and 44 percent of Asian students will eventually earn a bachelor's degree, only 7 percent of Latinos will do so (National Education Association 2001). This means that if we don't begin to turn this trend around, we will be in deep trouble.

Every morning, I am reminded of the urgency of this situation when I drive to work. I don't like to drive slowly so I have a transponder, or a Fast-Trak, that allows me to drive through a tollbooth under a device that reads my credit card information and charges my account. Even people without these transponders can drive through a separate lane that has an automated payment method; no service workers are involved in this.

My point is that the unskilled jobs and careers that require little or no education are disappearing fast and are being replaced with more technical, mentally demanding ones. At the same time, the fastest growing segment of our society is not attaining the education necessary to meet the changing needs of the American workplace.

In fact, according to the President's Advisory Commission on Educational Excellence for Hispanic Americans,

> By the year 2000, up to 80 percent of jobs in the United States are expected to require cognitive, rather than manual, skills, and 52 percent of jobs are expected to require at least some postsecondary education. The shortage of workers with high levels of communication, mathematics, computer and other technological skills—already a problem for employers—will become more severe, if the Hispanic population continues to be deprived of a quality education. (1996)

I feel the impact of these statistics every day and am aware that it is an awesome responsibility to assist my students in achieving their dreams. The concept of being a bridge between their present lives and the ones they wish to live in the future is what drives my teaching. However, when I first started teaching rigorously, I was unaware of this data. I simply did it because the thirty-odd kids sitting in my room every day trusted me. Now, when I consider that less than 10 percent of the Latino population finishes college, and only 54 percent even finish high school (Bowman 2005), I realize that I am part of a much bigger struggle.

If our workforce is not educationally equipped to meet the demands of the twenty-first century workplace, the cost of social programs and public-sponsored health care will skyrocket. Several states will experience a shrinking tax base, and the pressure to outsource skilled jobs will increase beyond resistance. This is a problem that affects all of us, no matter what part of the country we reside in.

Two days ago I looked out at my new Puente class, full of little ninth graders absurdly small and gangly for high school: Brenda nervously peeked out at the world from under the protective curtain of her carefully draped hair; Tony, with his crazy grin, flashed teeth, a bit too big for his face; Maggie, with her athletic, panther-like stride, entered the room ready for whatever came her way, but was nervous on the inside at the same time. These kids have been entrusted to me by society and by their parents. I cannot change the educational system, but I can change what happens to these kids who are my responsibility.

Thanks to the Puente program, I feel as if I have earned that trust. Since we introduced Puente to my high school, the rates of students eligible for the UC system have increased steadily. In 1999, only 12.5 percent of Puente graduates were UC eligible (Puente Project 2). By 2004, 43 percent of Puente graduates went on to actually attend a UC school, and 83 percent of the Puente graduates ended up at a four-year university (Magnolia High School WASC Accreditation Committee 2006). Also in 1999, for the very first time in Magnolia High School's forty-year history, a student was accepted to Harvard University: that student was a Puente graduate.

Our implementation of the Puente program has brought about other changes as well: 100 percent of my Puente students have passed our state's exit exam and the numbers of students in AP and Honors classes have swelled, as have the numbers of underrepresented students taking the SAT. More important, because of the changes Puente has effected on my campus, success is no longer the domain of the white and Asian kids; the overall culture of the school has changed.

Puente is an academic preparation or outreach program that is funded through the University of California. Although not limited to any one demographic, the class includes Latino literature and culture because the bulk of students tend to be Latino. The program operates in thirty-three high schools throughout California, and is headquartered in Oakland at the Office of the President for the UC system.

The program has no minimum GPA cutoff requirement and aims for a heterogeneous classroom with a wide range of student ability, motivation, and background. We incorporate a culturally responsive pedagogy into a rigorous curriculum aimed at preparing students for entrance to and success in a four-year university.

There are three main components to the Puente program at each high school. They include counseling, writing, and mentoring.

The first of these, counseling, is in place for all four years. Steve Gonzales, probably the hardest-working high school counselor I've ever met, works very closely with students through their high school career and is hugely responsible for the success of the program at Magnolia High School. As the Puente counselor, Steve oversees all the facets of student preparation for college—field trips to universities, PSAT and SAT registration, scholarship opportunities, leadership development, community service, and college applications. His work is never-ending. Seriously, someone needs to make a movie about this guy.

The second of these, writing, is in place for two years. At my site, Kelly Gallagher, author of *Reading Reasons* (2003), *Deeper Reading* (2004), and *Teaching Adolescent Writers* (2006), teaches one Puente class and I teach the other. The Puente students are enrolled in our Puente classes for their freshman and sophomore years and engage in a rigorous curriculum that highlights the various students' cultures. From there, about a fourth go on to Advanced Placement while the rest move on to regular English classes. However, our jobs with these students often extend beyond the first two years. Along with helping to plan field trips to universities, I also teach SAT preparation, work with students on scholarship essays, and offer guidance on the personal essay for the UC system. Although students are often out of my classroom after the second year, I am rarely out of their lives.

The third component of Puente is mentoring, which is arguably the most difficult to put into place. On our campus, ninth-grade students are paired up with eleventh-grade students and offered support with writing and study habits. This program sounds great in theory, but honestly works only sometimes. Also, the counselor and I make a concerted effort to bring back past students to share their college experiences with new students and to serve as role models for our students. This component has suffered the most, but it remains a part of the vision.

Statewide, Puente has much to be proud of, having benefited thousands of students. Of all the Latino students statewide who begin ninth grade, only a little over 3 percent of them will attend a UC (California Postsecondary Education Commission 2005). Yet, 23 percent of Puente students are UC eligible, making them twice as likely to be UC eligible as all non-Puente graduates of all backgrounds, and almost three times as likely to be UC eligible as other educationally disadvantaged graduates (23 percent versus 9 percent). Further, while only 49 percent of all California graduating high school seniors enter college, Puente students enter college at a rate of 79 percent (Puente Project 2007). Unlike some college preparation programs, Puente tracks its students beginning in the freshman year. If a student drops out of the program in the tenth grade, he or she is still counted in the data rather than being dropped. Therefore, these numbers are indicative of where our original thirty-odd students end up.

So, in a state where only 55 percent of Latinos and 66 percent of Latinas even graduate high school, how did Magnolia High School end up with a college-going rate of 83 percent? As Brenda Barajas, class of 2004, puts it,

> The structure of the Puente program was important, but the people working in the program had the biggest impact on me. Having a teacher and a counselor who really took the time to get to know my family and me, who were seriously devoted to the program's curriculum (and beyond it), and who were always seeking creative ways to reach out to students—that is what made Puente worthwhile for me. In the classroom, my teacher dared to challenge our class with AP level material and helped us with a SAT preparation course as well. He helped us to work together in groups, and to think as individuals. He even stayed after school to talk about intellectual ideas, things going on in our per-

sonal lives, or to watch a basketball game and thus put in the time to really get to know students. Similarly, my counselor's office was sort of like the "safe-haven" from the whirlwind of high school. Everyone sort of had like a daily check-in with him; we were always in his office. I remember spilling my heart to him on those stiff chairs, eating chocolates out of his candy bowl, and then receiving some announcement about an upcoming scholarship deadline. He would open his office before school, let us visit him between periods, and would stay there after-school often letting us use his computer to print out assignments or ap-plications. I think I even had my own folder on both of their computers! Both my counselor and teacher were dedicated to us as people, and professionally as students. I believe it was this combination that made the program one of my best experiences at Magnolia high school.

It is this approach to teaching and counseling that prompted researcher Helen Duffy to write, "Puente did more than simply tack on an additional literature in the way that some schools take on holiday and food celebrations in their attempts to acknowledge campus diversity. Puente altered the teacher-student relationship as a bridge to the acquisition of powerful academic discourse"(Duffy 2002). As mentioned before, the counseling component cannot be underemphasized when discussing the success of the Puente program at Magnolia High School. But this is a book about what happens in English class so in the chapters that follow, I'll deal with specific approaches to teaching literature and composition to students who traditionally have been underprepared for university success.

Interwoven through all these approaches is the belief that the student's background matters and that no two students come from the same place.

The current avalanche of test prep materials foisted upon an educational system saturated with the machinery of No Child Left Behind almost deliber-ately sidesteps an important fact: every day in our classrooms we are graced with thirty human beings, all of whom are much more complicated than we think, who often will not or cannot begin learning until we take the first step toward them. Students need to see teachers and counselors as willing partici-pants in their lives rather than as automatons forcing them to participate while in our institutions.

For underrepresented students, this issue is critical because many of them start high school without the knowledge or skill base necessary for academic success. Also, because of subtractive educational policies and the view that cultural diversity is a handicap rather than an asset, the school system stamps out students' desire to change and engage in a rigorous education. Like any salesperson, we educators must connect to who our students are before they will "buy" our product; to do this, we must become students of their culture.

The second principle is that no two students come from the same place. Just because a student is from a particular ethnic group does not mean that he or she will be like other students from that group. Culture does not work like that—we are all invested in dozens of subcultures that work together to shape our behavior. A student may be more influenced by his membership in the surfing subculture than his Mexican heritage, for instance. As a result, there is no one approach that will work with any one ethnic background.

However, there are ways that educators can adjust their practices so that students of all backgrounds can succeed and go on to higher education. The remaining chapters of this book aim to weave sound pedagogical practices with the attention that culture needs to receive in a classroom full of underrepresented students. By doing so, the education a student receives improves. As Italia Lima, a former Puentista who is now at UC Davis, puts it,

> Puente opened my eyes to my cultural roots, allowed me to bridge relationships with instructors and peers, and unlocked the fascinating world of college life. My studies at UC Davis have opened my eyes to the inequalities low-resource youths have when applying to a four-year institution. For some, the admission process serves as a barrier for success, sending them into the abyss of menial employment. Luckily for some, acceptance to a university hides behind a devoted counselor, supporting teacher, and a successful program that still believes in the power of education. Now two years into my college career, I have grown into an individual that wouldn't have existed if it weren't for Puente. I'm fully devoted to my passions: my studies, serving the greater good in my communities, and most importantly, the ability to believe that anything can be conquered.

When my time with my freshmen is over, I want them to have experienced so much more than just an increase in their test scores. Scores need to improve of course, but education is so much deeper than that. By beginning with the student and his or her culture, I can reach much further into my students' lives and help them see *why* they want to continue their education. As a result, my classroom becomes a place where lives are changed and dreams are pursued and where I get the fulfillment of being part of a team that operates as a bridge between where the students are and where they wish to end up; that's the reason why I chose this profession to begin with.

This book draws greatly from my experience in the Puente classroom, but its applications are not limited to the program. Everything that I have learned has spilled over into my other classes—I am a better instructor overall because of my Puente training. As educational researcher G. M. Pradl writes, "The rigorous college preparatory English curriculum that anchors High School Puente merits serious attention by education policy makers because its core principles . . . apply beyond the Mexican American/Latino student population for which it was originally designed . . . Puente offers an encouraging model for working with underserved students whatever their ethnic, cultural, or socio-economic origins" (Pradl 2002). In other words, although Puente emphasizes Latino literature and culture, the principle of acknowledging the cultural capital that underrepresented students possess rather than treating it as an obstacle to be overcome can be applied to any ethnic group or other subculture within a school. Puente pedagogy—emphasizing a student's culture—works beyond solely Latino populations, a necessary focus if we want our future workforce to sustain its competitiveness and achieve its dreams.

CHAPTER TWO

Familia and Classroom Culture

I LOOK OVER AT MY TEN-YEAR-OLD SON, SQUINTING AGAINST THE WIND AS WE RACE IN MY CONVERTIBLE TO HIS FIRST DAY OF LITTLE LEAGUE PRACTICE. JARED IS ON A NEW TEAM AND I WORRY ABOUT HIM BEING THROWN INTO A NEW GROUP OF BOYS QUITE DIFFERENT FROM THE ONE HE WAS USED TO.

WHEN I MEET THE OTHER PARENTS, I CAN QUICKLY SENSE THAT THIS TEAM HAS A DIFFERENT FEEL TO IT AND REFLECTS A SOMEWHAT DIFFERENT CULTURE; MOST OF THE KIDS ARE FROM AN OLDER, MORE BLUE-COLLAR NEIGHBORHOOD.

On the first afternoon of practice, I show up with Jared, who watches from the sidelines for a few minutes before warming up. The coach, Scott Fossum, has a reputation for demanding a lot from the kids and their parents and sometimes finds himself in conflict with other coaches and officials. He towers over the kids, his shaven, muscled skull glistening with sweat, his fading goatee giving him a rough-hewn look. His eyes are full of passion and nervous energy—clearly, this man is all baseball.

I glance nervously at my son. He seems so fragile at this moment. He has average skills as a ball player, and I'm not convinced that this will be a positive experience for him.

Then Coach Fossum opens his mouth and begins to explain how today's drill, the first in a long season, will be conducted. Expecting him to discuss either the mechanics of hitting or the correct stance to assume when throwing, I am surprised when he introduces his very first lesson: "Today," he says, smiling wickedly, "we start with the very first step toward becoming champions: treating each other like family."

With that, I know my son is in for a great season of baseball, led by a great coach who will knit his players together into a family. By working together for a common goal, they will capture the title of the Lake Forest Lake League champions at the season's end.

Many of the underrepresented students in my classroom enter school feeling like Jared, the newcomer on the team. The trepidation my son felt when he first met Fossum is not dissimilar to how many of my students feel when they first meet me. The thesis of this book is that educators need to approach teaching in the same manner with which Fossum approaches coaching: with total passion, making high demands, providing plenty of encouragement, and emphasizing a shared sense of community. Tony Dungy, the first African American football coach to win a Super Bowl, shares this view, stating,

> For years and years in the NFL the coach had to project a certain image. You very much had to be someone who intimidated people. You've got these big brutish guys and they only stay in line if they're afraid of the coach. If the coach isn't somebody who can control them, then they're not going to perform. So when I talked about going in and getting the right type of guys, and we're going to win 'cause we're going to create a family atmosphere where they're going to really like each other and play for each other, well, not everybody related to that. (Starr 2007)

So many successful coaches, teachers, and businessmen understand the importance of creating a team spirit that feels like a family, or *familia,* as we say in my Puente classroom.

Bringing my students together as a family increases their chances of success—the assistance and encouragement they get from each other helps anchor some that might otherwise be distracted from their long-term dreams by short-term temptations.

Unlike my son, who loves sports, I never succeeded in athletics as a child. A few years ago, I went rock climbing for the first time, fully expecting to fail miserably. However, once I got started, my friends encouraged me greatly, saying, "good move," or "nice job." They offered tips and suggestions as well, pointing out possible moves that my inexperienced eyes could not see. Soon, I was basking in the sun, feeling a cool wind envelop me as I stood at the literal summit of my accomplishment. I enjoyed succeeding at that first fairly easy attempt, and so I went on to challenge myself with more difficult climbs. Gradually, my sense that I was a non-athlete faded, erased by the encouragement of my friends, who formed my nuclear rock-climbing community. After a few more climbs over the next several months, I purchased climbing shoes and some of the necessary gear and joined a rock-climbing gym. I have never forgotten that first day of rock climbing, and every September when I teach a new batch of freshmen, I am reminded of it.

This September, I begin the school year watching a group of freshmen meander in. They look wide-eyed and nervous, and I can almost hear them thinking, *I don't belong here.* So many of my students feel like they do not belong in the academic world, that reading and writing are for students who look different or come from different ethnic backgrounds. For me to have any lasting effect on underserved students, I must effect a paradigm shift on them: they need to think of themselves as writers. Also, if a non-athlete like me can think of himself as a rock climber after just a few short months, my students can certainly make a similar change in their self-perception as well, just as long as I offer encouragement and facilitate a community atmosphere, offer plenty of tips and suggestions as they grow, and let them succeed at simpler tasks before moving them on to more complex challenges.

Familia and Culture at the Beginning of the School Year

It is early September as I write this, and school has been in session for two days. During that time I have attempted to create a sense of *familia* in the classroom, emphasizing our common mission: to help the students get into a four-year university and succeed once they get there. This concept of *familia* permeates every activity of the class.

Before my students enter the classroom, I make sure that the room conveys the right message to them. The desks are arranged such that there is no "back of the class"—all thirty-seven desks face each other in a U-shaped configuration that grants me easy access to all my students. Pictures of students adorn the walls, as do collages from the last sixteen years.

I have also put up Reading Charts (logs of the time students spent reading outside of class), charts depicting the Writing Process, explanatory posters on the domains of writing, various informative charts on college (required courses for Cal State and UC schools, scholarships, etc.), and quotations about college from other students.

The message is inescapable here: this is a classroom that celebrates students while focusing intensely on reading, writing, and preparation for university. Indeed, as my freshmen begin to walk in, I watch them study the classroom and me, trying to figure out what the class will be like.

Next, I initiate a major step in the creation of *familia* in the class: I plan to learn the names of all my students by the end of the first class meeting. To begin, I inform them that each desk has a Post-it note with a student's name on it, and their first task is to find their desk. The names are arranged in alphabetical order according to each student's first name. Once the students are seated, I know that those students to my left have first names from the beginning of the alphabet and that those to my right have names that start with the last few letters. This makes it easy for me to know their names before the end of the class.

Similarly, I want them to know each other's names as well so on the first day, I avoid an endless lecture on classroom rules and I do not spend much time on the syllabus. Instead, we read and we write. In groups of three, students read letters from last year's students and note what their predecessors have said about the class and how to succeed in it. Each group subsequently shares its findings with the whole class. By the end of the first fifty-minute class, students have begun to know me a little, we have worked together to some degree, they are aware that I know them by name, we have done reading and writing exercises, and we have felt somewhat connected to a classroom that has a legacy of helping students achieve their dreams. By doing so, I have taken the first step toward creating the feeling of *familia*.

During the first two weeks, I make sure that at least once we have former students visit to speak briefly to the freshmen. This September, Brenda, a student at Stanford University, visited us. One student reflected on his view of *familia:* "the idea that they [past students] are going to go to college and then come back and help with later generations is emphasized when past students come back to talk to us or e-mail us about college."

By the end of the second week, my students have heard much from past Puente students, and the more my freshmen hear from past students who have gone on to be successful, the more they feel plugged into something important and worthwhile. As Jovanna, an enthusiastic freshman, puts it,

> We speak openly, share thoughts and opinions. We have a sort of confidence to be ourselves and enjoy others. It's not all education we work together in, although it's the main reason why we're here, but it's the things that come with it, the people you're surrounded by, the support and the fun and jokes we do to start our day off great.

When students feel valued and that their voice and their world matter, they feel comfortable enough to take risks they would otherwise not attempt. As one student wrote, "Family doesn't judge family." The more my students bring their own home lives into the classroom, the more ownership they feel over the curriculum and their own writing skills. As Edgar, my quiet, studious future college student, says, "We are getting to know each other closely, and we are able to share stories about our lives."

This, then, is where my Puente class begins: with the underlying assumption that students' cultural backgrounds matter. The various subcultures that they belong to—pertaining to ethnicity, class, sports, hobbies, music—all these aspects of their lives matter and should be valued appropriately. The students also know that they are part of a chain of success. Those who have moved on from Magnolia High School and into higher education frequently come back to share their experiences and provide encouragement and support.

Discussing the concept of establishing a culture of *familia,* Cuper wrote the following:

> From my perspective, I think the concept of "familia" is that we are helping each

other get toward a university and once we get there, we will come back and help our community and each other once again.

Honestly, what educator wouldn't want a room full of energetic ninth graders filled with this sense of mission?

The Birth Order Essay

Reflecting on his writing skills, Danny wrote, "We approach writing in this class with strength and bravery. The strength is we work hard on every paper. Bravery because we are not afraid to write things that are personal and we're not afraid to make mistakes." In working with underrepresented students, I present a quick introduction to writing and the writing process in my freshman English class. For their first assignment, I want to focus on the students yet keep the writing academic so I have used birth order research (BOR) as a springboard for the paper. In a nutshell, students examine how birth order research describes their personalities and then decide whether or not they agree, providing specific examples from their lives to support their view. It is a basic expository piece of writing that I present fairly quickly, using it to teach the writing process. It also helps facilitate a sense of *familia* because it requires students to share their stories with each other through the writing of the paper. This section is dedicated to explaining how I present the birth order information.

During the first week of school, I explain what birth order research is and how the terms are defined. I begin by having students list all their siblings, including themselves, along with their ages. Half-brothers and half-sisters and step-brothers and step-sisters count if they live(d) with the student for a substantial time and a definite relationship exists.

Next, students are to delete the names of anyone more than five years older or younger than themselves (BOR stipulates that anything more than five years' difference doesn't have enough influence on the child to affect much behavior). Also, twins or siblings with special needs are automatically assigned the "Youngest Child" designation. Students write down which term describes them: oldest child, middle child, youngest child, or only child, keeping in mind that siblings more than five years apart in age should not be included in this list.

Students meet according to their birth order designation (first-born, middle, youngest, only children) and arrange their desks in a circle. Although I do not place much stock in BOR, I have noticed over the years that the "Oldest Child" group usually forms a nearly perfect circle and awaits instructions, whereas the "Youngest Child" circle is often disorderly, noisy, and unfocused.

I place a folded sheet of paper that says "Read Me" on the floor in the middle of each group. Almost always, the first-born group gets right to work reading the instructions, whereas the last-born group takes a while longer to get going, sometimes not even noticing the paper on the ground.

When the paper is unfolded, students in the last-born group see that the instructions are to "Brainstorm or list traits that last-borns have in common." Similar instructions are printed on the papers for the other groups. Taking the allotted ten minutes I give them, the students quickly list traits that they have in common on one sheet of paper. As I walk around the room, I cannot help but notice how frequently the students' behavior reflects the conclusion of much BOR: my first-borns are assigning who will write down the list, the middle-borns are negotiating, often with every group member writing his or her own copy of the list, and the last-borns are arguing over who has to write it out. There is much more laughter coming from the last-born group, a lot of discussion from the middle-born, and the first-born is fairly quiet yet on task.

I have each group put their list on the ELMO, a data-capturing tool connected to an LCD projector, allowing me to project student work immediately onto a screen to share their findings with the rest of the class. I then reveal what the actual research says, findings that I have included later in this section, and ask each group to take notes on the applicable information.

All this takes about fifty minutes, which is an entire class period at my school. The next day, I ask students to make a T-chart: on the left, they are required to write an aspect of the research; on the right, they must write an example from their own lives that reflects the accuracy or inaccuracy of the research. My example is shown in Figure 2.1.

Figure 2.1 Research and Evidence T-Chart

What the Research Says	Evidence Showing Accuracy / Inaccuracy
» Can be a procrastinator to relieve burden of perfectionism	When I did a workshop at Berkeley this summer, I waited until the weekend before to start putting my ideas together—projects like organizing my CDs and cleaning my garage seemed more important.
» Cold-blooded	Once when my daughter dropped her ice cream cone and started crying, I laughed because it looked so funny.
» Well-organized	My files for teaching are in chronological order (the hard copies) and arranged in folders on my computer. My CDs are in alphabetical order by artist.
» Standing out in their field in some way	I enjoy doing workshops and training other teachers.

In class, I present the above chart to my students before they create their own. The question I pose to the class is, "Which piece of evidence seems the most vague to you?" The last one ("I enjoy doing workshops and training other teachers") is lacking in specificity. I then ask, "How could I make it more specific?" to which the students respond by suggesting I discuss specific workshops or training sessions I have conducted. So I add, "For the past seven years I've conducted Puente training sessions during the summer, presenting techniques that I've developed."

Students will then decide how accurate BOR is about themselves, and will list specific examples from their own lives that support their views. I use this very quick paper to teach the writing process, writing competencies, and a few basic skills (such as specificity of evidence). The actual prompt that the students write to is as follows:

In a well-written paper, argue how accurately birth order research describes you. Use evidence from your own life to support your thesis.

As we work through the paper, I begin creating a scoring guide with them. At first, I list only one thing: a clear thesis. As I go through mini-lessons on some of the aspects of writing discussed in the following sections, I add descriptors to the scoring guide. By the end of the week, I have the actual scoring guide complete and give it to each student. The finished scoring guide is shown below.

Birth Order Paper Scoring Guide

EXCELLENT WRITING:
- Sophisticated thesis statement
- Paper remains focused on thesis throughout
- Insightful discussion throughout the paper
- Large amount of specific evidence from the writer's own life
- Skillful use of transitions
- Collegiate tone, vocabulary
- Effective sentence branching
- Successful editing of ambitious writing

VERY GOOD WRITING:
- Strong thesis statement
- Paper remains generally focused on thesis throughout
- Somewhat consistent insightful discussion throughout the paper
- Use of specific evidence from the writer's own life
- Effective use of transitions
- Somewhat consistent collegiate tone and vocabulary
- Successful sentence branching
- Generally free of editing mistakes in somewhat ambitious writing

GOOD WRITING:
- Clear thesis statement
- Paper remains focused on thesis for most of paper
- Adequate discussion throughout the paper
- While most evidence is specific, writer should include more evidence OR
- Writer includes much evidence but should work on specificity in places
- Adequate use of transitions with mixed consistency
- While tone and vocabulary are not collegiate, they are mature
- Sentence branching could be increased/improved
- Some editing mistakes, but generally successful editing of adequate writing

23

POTENTIALLY GOOD WRITING:

- Unclear thesis statement
- Paper wanders from the thesis on a few occasions
- Discussion throughout the paper needs more reflection
- More specific evidence needed from the writer's own life
- Inconsistent or incorrect use of transitions
- Some instances where writer uses slang or non-academic language
- Some instances where sentence branching would improve paper
- Several passages that require further editing

REQUIRED REWRITE:

- Unclear or missing thesis statement
- Paper wanders from thesis on several occasions
- Discussion throughout the paper only restates research without writer's opinions OR
- Discussion throughout the paper only states writer's opinions without stating research
- No transitions
- Several instances where writer uses slang or non-academic language
- Several passages that require further editing; sentence boundaries need work OR
- Some passages difficult to understand because of editing that still needs to be done

I like doing the paper because the material being discussed is personal but discussed as an expository discourse. Also, I feel that it helps me to get to know my students very quickly because they are basically describing their personalities in this assignment. Whether or not the research is accurate is, of course, immaterial; I only care that they begin to understand the writing process and to develop writing skills.

In the next several chapters, I will discuss the major papers that we write—keep in mind that the birth order assignment is presented in class very fast (usually over about two weeks); it is an expository paper that gives me a glimpse of my students' personalities and writing abilities at the beginning of the year.

What follows includes the information on BOR that I present in my classes:

First-born Child

PERSONALITY TRAITS
- Achiever, highly motivated, in control, self-sacrificing, goal-oriented, well-organized, self-reliant, tolerant, patient
- Compliant and wanting to please *or* strong-willed and aggressive
- Legalistic, overbearing, stubborn, sees things as either "black or white," unforgiving, holds grudges

MENTAL TRAITS
- Precise, strong powers of concentration, mental discipline, analytical, serious, critical, scholarly
- Skeptical, cynical, sarcastic, close-minded

WORK TRAITS
- Perfectionistic, reliable, conscientious, punctual, list maker

TYPICAL CAREERS
- Science, medicine, law, accountancy, bookkeeping, executive secretary, engineering, computer science
- Go on to positions of leadership or high achievement (52 percent of U.S. presidents were first-born children)
- Overrepresented among *Who's Who in America*, Rhodes Scholars, university professors

STRONG BELIEFS
- Supportive of law and order, authority, loyalty, protocol

Middle Child

PERSONALITY TRAITS
- Completely unlike first-born child
- Mediator, negotiator, independent, monogamous
- Prone to embarrassment, misunderstood, secretive

SOCIAL TRAITS
- Avoids conflict, extremely loyal to friends, has many friends
- Out of place, often willing to "give in"

FAMILIAL TRAITS
- Feels "left out" within family, has very few pictures of family members

TYPICAL CAREERS
- Career path almost always in stark contrast to that of a first-born child
- Managers, leaders, jobs involving compromise and negotiation

STRONG BELIEF
- Relationships, people

Youngest Child

PERSONALITY TRAITS
- Charming, shows off, people person, precocious, affectionate, uncomplicated, carefree, vivacious
- Rebellious, critical, temperamental, impatient, impetuous, manipulative, blames others, somewhat absentminded

TYPICAL CAREERS
- Sales, professions that require the ability to be "on stage" and to perform
- Show business

MOTIVATING FACTORS
- Praise and encouragement, "do it now and worry later," short-term rewards

Only Child

PERSONALITY TRAITS
- Gets along well with those older or younger (but not same age), reliable and conscientious, well-organized, cautious, conservative, likes to be a "rescuer"
- May procrastinate to relieve burden of perfectionism
- Difficulty relating to peers, self-centered, cold-blooded

MENTAL TRAITS
- Critical of self and others; serious, scholarly, objective

TYPICAL CAREERS
- Same as oldest child, except to a greater extent; prominent in chosen field in some way; career choices include science, medicine, law, accounting, bookkeeping, executive secretaries, engineering, computer science.
- These individuals go beyond the boundaries of a given field or create new boundaries.

DIFFERENCES BETWEEN "ONLY" AND "FIRST-BORN" CHILDREN
- Most characteristics are the same; however, only children are more extreme in most characteristics common to first-borns.

Sample Paper—Birth Order Research

I use student samples with almost every paper my students write, to model responses and to impart a sense of how to evaluate their own writing. Ozzy's paper, which follows, was a good one to use this year because it has much that is praiseworthy and much that needs improvement. He begins with an ordinary introduction that simply states his thesis (I will teach them how to write an introduction later in the semester), and backs it up with specific evidence. I point out his overuse of the word *I* in the paper and some editing changes that need to be made. Although Ozzy is a beginning writer, his enthusiasm and

27

willingness to experiment with language make me optimistic that he will do well in the class; also, he enjoys the public response to his paper.

OSWALDO RAMIREZ
SEPTEMBER 27, 2006
PERIOD 2
BIRTH ORDER RESEARCH

The birth order research describes my personality accurately.

Some of the examples that the research depicted was based on academic area. To demonstrate, one of those named was scholarly. An example of this is that I made it into Oxford Academy, one of the most prestigic high schools in southern California. Also, I started the GATE program since I've been in second grade. Another trait listed for first bournes was being a perfectionist. To illustrate, last week I had to clean my room, one of my favorite places to be, so I made sure everything was juts the way I wanted it to be. Likewise, last time I had to write an essay, I made sure I followed every single instruction and direction given. Stating that there are occasions where I try to be a perfectionist.

The research done concluded that traits were not always positive, such as a trait described as holding grudges. For instance, in my last football game against Orange High, I got into a fight with #2. After every play, no matter where it ended in the field, I would be right in his face. Even though the game ended two weeks ago, I still hold a grudge for the player with the #2. In the same way I have also held a grudge against a dog. I went to my cousins house for our weekly gathering. I found out that my cousin had gotten a new puppy. Regardless of how cute the puppy looked, it was a vicious dog. I tried to pet it but it snapped at me and had bitten me. That is how my grudge against that dog started. Another negative trait is being in control. An example of this is that every single time I go to the movies with my friends, I always get to see the movie I want to. In retrospect, first born children do have negative traits.

The next couple of traits can be listed under maturity. For example, one of those traits described in the research was being serious. An example would also have to do with the last time I saw a movie. My friends and I watched "Gridiron Gang". All of my friends were messing around and I noticed there were a lot of people, mostly mature, watching us. So I tried to be serious while being with them so it doesn't make everyone look that bad. Similarly, there have been times when we have a substitute teacher and all of the other students start messing around. A lot of them must think we are excused from the rules. So usually in these situations is when I try to be the most serious and professional as possible. Again the next trait would go under maturity would be being reliable. There are several occasions when I am relied on by my family and other people as well. One of the most important times I get relied on is when I play football specifically when the coach gives me the plays to remember to give to the rest of the team, one of the best freshman teams that Magnolia High has ever seen. If I happened to forget the play, I have just messed up one play that could have possibly given us a touchdown. In a like a manner, there are also times when I run errands for my mother, which I despise doing. If she tells to go to Ralphs to pick up some things and she only gives me a certain amount of money, she relies on me to give her all the change. The reason for me being relied on is because last time my sister was sent she spent all the change she was supposed to give back. Therefore, I am the one in charge of being given the pressure.

There all still several other traits that have depicted my personality accurately according to the birth order research.

A Culture of Writing: Modeling Effective Writing

I used to hate Christmas Eve; every year it was the same—a lengthy gift-opening process, followed by a long drive home with two very tired children, followed by an all-night session of assembling all the toys. One year we bought bicycles for each of our two children and had to put them together in the middle of the night without making any noise. Thank God the instructions included pictures of what each stage was supposed to look like. Without the visual example of the finished product, I'm pretty sure my daughter's bike would have collapsed right after its first jump off the curb. I envy the fathers in my neighborhood who intuitively know how to put together bicycles and swing sets, and especially the fathers who can build their own decks; projects like those always make me feel inadequate.

Similarly, I think that many of my students feel insecure about their writing skills, and that they need a visual example of what their finished product ought to look like in order to produce a college-level essay.

It is very important to model effective writing to underserved students. Many of my students have incredible potential but lack the resources at home that can provide direction and guidance when it comes to writing; several students have parents who do not even speak English. Therefore, providing samples is essential, and I recommend that for every piece of writing that you teach, students should see several examples of varying approaches and skill levels. Simple directions for writing pale in comparison to the power of seeing examples.

Further, when assigning a paper, there is no substitute for writing it yourself, or at least putting together a first draft. There are so many insights to my writing assignments that I have gleaned from doing them myself, so I am a zealous believer in writing as many of the papers I assign as possible, especially if I am not getting the student results I want. I know how crazy this sounds, given our busy teaching schedules, but writing the assignments with my students helps me to anticipate difficulties my writers will experience and therefore helps to tailor my teaching to avoid the pitfalls inherent in any writing assignment.

In my Advanced Placement class, nearly every year I do an actual timed writing with the students, using a laptop and an LCD projector. I narrate as I write so that my students see what goes through my mind as I formulate my ideas, compose my argument, and then briefly revise and edit my essay. It is a very nerve-wracking experience, but it is also one of the most beneficial.

Along with providing good samples from a variety of sources (professional, your own, past students), it is also helpful to run scoring sessions from time to time. I usually pull a range of papers from the previous year and make a class set of them. Here's the basic format I tend to follow:

READ THROUGH SCORING GUIDE
- Read sample paper as a class.
- Share score/grade for sample paper.
- Have students read a second paper individually.
- Ask students to score/grade the second paper individually.
- Ask students to discuss their scores/grades in small groups.
- Poll the class to see how they scored/graded the second paper.
- Discuss their assessment of the second paper and of what they could do to improve the paper.
- Share actual score/grade with class.
- Continue these steps with more student assignments.

I usually ask students to read an average paper to begin with, then have them read and score a second sample. I usually follow the pattern of individual scoring, then discussing with a partner/small group, then class discussion. I actually go around the room and ask students to vote on how they would score a paper.

Conclusion

Adolescents today are starved for a sense of community, and they will find it somewhere—it is to our advantage as educators to inculcate that feeling of community in the classroom. I have never been as convinced of this as recently when some of my students explained the wonder of MySpace to me. For those unfamiliar with the site, teenagers create a web page about themselves, including pictures, blogs, mottos, and other personal information, which other teens then look at, comment on, and reply to. After Yahoo!, MySpace is the number two website in the United States, worth over six billion dollars and with over one hundred million accounts. It is growing at about 500,000 new accounts a week (Cashmore 2006). Its secret is that it creates community for its users. As one student, Jovanna Nolazco, puts it,

> MySpace gives people the opportunity to choose who they want to talk to, who they can put on their page. It's like your own little community. All the people on your page are people who you know you like and want to talk to. There's something so intriguing about having all your favorite people on one page and being able to talk to them all day.

The need to belong is so strong in this digitized generation that to facilitate a sense of community, or *familia,* can be a powerful motivating force for adolescents. In my class I try to never lose sight of the students who otherwise would get lost and be forgotten in the classroom—too often, such a student is the underrepresented student—and instead, I actively work to draw those students into the mainstream of the class. Learning and using my students' names within the first two days, creating a seating arrangement that leaves no one stranded in a corner, getting kids to interact on a near-daily basis, and conveying messages purposefully with the displays on my classroom walls—

these are some of the techniques I use to accomplish *familia* in the classroom. Here are ten quick ways to help foster the concept of *familia*:

1. Take pictures of your students at prom, sporting events, assemblies, in class, and other places and post them in your classroom.
2. Try to find something to talk about with each student—their job, sports, clubs, hobbies, or music. A quick moment or two of conversation about something personal can make a lasting impact on a student.
3. Display student work on your walls.
4. Teach students how to have a classroom discussion. Have them use each other's names in conversation. Make sure your students know each other's names.
5. Bring back past students for quick talks of how your class has benefited them. Let your students see that they are part of a community of students who have gone on to be successful.
6. Set up writing groups as soon as possible. Have your students react to student work as quickly as possible. In an English class, it isn't enough to be a community; we need to be a community of readers and writers with plans for future academic success.
7. Let students see that you are part of their community. Laugh at their jokes, show them your own struggles with writing, and listen to their criticism of your own writing.
8. Listen to students' music during writing time after previewing the lyrics.
9. Make time outside the classroom to foster community. This past year, I have used my lunch break to play cards, video games, and Pictionary with my students, and have spent after-school time to eat hamburgers and attend plays, bonfires, and movies with groups of students.
10. When conferring with a student about a paper, suggest another student to look at it as well. A community of writers is the goal here.

The most important thing I have learned is to be interested in my students. I have found that if I start with that, everything else falls into place. The passion, intensity of caring, and demand for teamwork that my son's Little League coach displays during game time are the same qualities that I need to exhibit when I teach. It is not enough to simply go through the motions of learning; students need to truly acquire the skills required for the twenty-first century.

In Ron Ritchart's *Intellectual Character: What It Is, Why It Matters, and How to Get It*, he argues that teachers can either emphasize effort (do all the work, earn an A) when they grade or they can shape their students' dispositions. He contrasts classrooms in which "students complete work rather than learn" with those that develop thinking (Ritchart 2004). Within the first two weeks of school, my goal is to create an environment in which I emphasize the concept of *familia* centered on the pursuit of skills and a healthy disposition toward writing, and indeed, thinking.

One final note: the creation of community in an English classroom needs to be infused with a sense of purpose. In my classes, that means that the very real fact that the students need my class and the skills it emphasizes—reading, writing, thinking—gets reinforced on a near-daily basis. We do our underrepresented students no favors if we simply make them feel good for a school year. The goal needs to be to enable them to successfully cross the bridge from high school to higher learning, and the odds of that taking place increase substantially if we facilitate the formation of a community of readers, writers, and thinkers.

CHAPTER THREE

Literary Analysis: Reading and Writing Strategies

Bawja	Koppelman	Sima
Cabuhat	Lee	Sinoy
Chance	Leeser	Todora
Choa	Leon*	Tran
Faoa	Liv	Warren
Galasso	Pham	Wu
Hernandez*	Pharis	Young
Howell	Ramirez*	
Kim	Shim	

These are the last names on the roster of my very first honors class, which I taught in 1998. The high school was over 50 percent Latino at the time, and yet Latinos were almost nowhere to be found in the most rigorous courses (Latino last names are marked with an asterisk in this list and the one that follows). In the 1990s, the honors classes fed directly into Advanced Placement (AP) classes, and beginning in elementary school, the same thirty or so students went on to take the highest level of classes together. The honors and AP class rolls did not reflect the demographics of the school at all, which is probably true in all too many schools across the nation.

To combat this, Puente began focusing on ways to prepare underrepresented students in the ninth and tenth grades so that they would be capable of success in the most challenging classes offered in high school. The organization trained its teachers in pre-AP strategies and emphasized the importance of enabling students to enroll and succeed in such rigorous classes. As a result of this process, here are the last names from my roster of AP class of 2005:

Alcala*	Gutierrez*	Ortega*
Brown	Harada	Ortiz*
Bueno*	Hernandez*	Patel
Camarena*	Jones	Phan
Canizales*	Kan	Pinedo*
Clausi	Kindell	Reynon
Cossio*	Mai	Stephens
Faircloth	Marina	Tapia*
Garner	Middleton	Tran
Guerra*	Nguyen	Uribe*

In the past three years at Magnolia High School, 43 Latinos have completed AP English. The students with asterisks next to their names in the above list would probably have been left out of AP English ten years ago because of tracking and the failure of the school system to prepare average students for the more rigorous honors and AP classes. Today, most of these students have passed both AP English Language and AP English Literature exams; many of them have gone on to be successful students at schools like UC Berkeley and UCLA.

That kind of success with underrepresented students occurred only after a team of teachers and counselors began to fill many of the cracks that our college-bound kids fall through too often—increasing the number of students taking the SATs, providing assistance with college applications and essays, increasing access to scholarship information, and the focus of this chapter, increasing student preparedness for AP classes.

Going through this process has led me to realize that the education business is made up of two kinds of people: idealists and pragmatists. A good teacher, I think, has to have a healthy dose of both qualities. I am optimistic that underrepresented students, given the right tools, will overcome many of the obstacles that stand in their way and will develop a love for reading and the written exchange of ideas. I am driven by this belief. My students have placed their trust in me and in the public school system; they honestly think, deep down, that we all have their best interests at heart. That trust in me compels me to give them the very best education possible, and I am idealistic about the importance of the role I play in my students' lives.

However, the pragmatist in me pushes me to examine the educational landscape my underserved students must wade through as they make the journey toward their goals. For instance, in 2003 only 4,300 students were admitted to UCLA out of 40,700 applicants. Those admitted boasted an average 4.13 GPA and an average SAT I score of 1278. They took, on average, 17 semesters of honors courses in high school as well (Lin-Eftekhar and Mack 2003). The competition to get into good universities has never been so brutal, nor have the skills required for college success been so rigorous, which requires students today to tread carefully through the terrain of high school. Thus, the importance of honors and AP classes, or of the ability to succeed on the SAT, or the Exit Exam, cannot be discounted. I could not live with myself if I facilitated students' finding their voice in their writing but let them fail the Exit Exam in my state.

To be honest, much of my time with my students is spent straddling the fence that divides the idealists from the pragmatists. For instance, although I doubt that the SAT for Critical Reading truly measures a student's skill level, I realize the importance of preparing students for the exam. Without that extra preparation, students whose ability levels reflect the potential for academic success will nevertheless see the doors to many universities slam shut. Therefore, every year I scramble for funding to provide an SAT preparation class for our hundred or so students who want to go on to college. However, I don't think that the preparation class truly makes anyone a better reader or writer, which may be a sign of the tension between the idealist and the pragmatist in me.

From the start, one of my goals for my Puente students is to instill in them the joy of reading complex and thought-provoking texts; in fact, this is the foundation of my instruction. I also realize that it is my duty to help them acquire the writing skills that will allow them to articulate their ideas about complex and thought-provoking texts. Next, I try to equip as many of my students as possible for the rigors of AP classes. Some students choose not to make the jump to AP, and I believe that they are better served and better equipped for success because of having been exposed to higher-level thinking skills and advanced reading and writing techniques. Access to AP courses opens doors for my students now and in the future, which is why I work so strenuously on the written analysis of literature.

Thus, it is clear that we can ignore neither the idealistic notion that all students should organically develop an appreciation for reading and writing nor the pragmatic necessity of equipping our students with the tools necessary to succeed in the academic culture of the twenty-first century.

Reading the Details

When I first began teaching, I did not understand the meaning of the word *analysis*. I thought it meant to think deeply about something, and I hear many teachers use it in this manner. However, to analyze something is to break it down into its parts. Good literary analysis breaks down the text, examines the parts, and creates interpretations based on those examinations. In teaching literary analysis to underrepresented students, I am always aware of the fact that many of my students are starting from square one, and that every aspect of good literary analysis—how to integrate quotes, how to balance textual evidence with their own thinking, how to synthesize and analyze the words and sentences in a text—must be explicitly taught. Simply assigning the paper and hoping for the best will not work with students who are mostly new to this style of writing. So I start with the very basics when teaching analysis to my students.

Excited to begin on this road, I ask my students to close their eyes and tell them that I am about to say a sentence that I want them to visualize with as much detail as possible: *He bellowed*.

"Got that image in your mind?" Sixteen heads bob in unison. Estephanie looks at me with a quizzical expression. It does seem like an odd moment in the classroom. "Okay, here's my question to you: how much did the man weigh?"

Estephanie answers, "Like 300 pounds" and Joe responds, "A lot." I ask the class how many of them imagined someone overweight, and most of the hands spring up into the air. "Why is that? There's nothing in that sentence that indicates weight; it's just a male making a loud noise."

Joe responds that the word *bellows* sounds "like a sound a cow would make" while another student responds that it is a walrus noise. Many of the students look at each other, surprised that they all saw the same basic image. I tell them that "the verb *bellows* means to shout, roar, or holler, but it also suggests that someone overweight is making the noise. This extra suggestion is not found in the dictionary; it's what we English teachers like to call *connotation*. The word *bellows* connotes heaviness.

"Let's try another one," I say, and the students quickly close their eyes; Estephanie begins to laugh. "Clear your mind of the first guy, close your eyes, and imagine this sentence: *He shrieked*." Here, the students kind of laugh at the image. I quickly ask, "What did he look like?"

"Skinny and weak," responds Joe. I ask how many saw the same image, and once again, most of the students raise their hands. I say, "That's what most students think. The word *shrieked* connotes weakness or fragility."

Next, I move on to a couple of other plays with connotation. For instance, the word *pierce* means to poke a hole in something (like getting your ears pierced). The word *puncture* means to poke a hole in something (like puncturing a tire). I ask my students to consider the following two sentences:

Love pierced his heart.

Love punctured his heart.

Here's my question: In which instance did the man fall in love and in which instance did the man have his heart broken? After my students discuss this briefly in pairs, Joanna responds that "the guy in love is the one with the pierced heart." Most of the other heads in the classroom nod in agreement. I tell them that they are correct, that *pierced* carries a positive connotation, while *punctured* carries a negative connotation—think of how gentle and precise piercing is versus how violent puncturing is.

Estephanie leans back, smiling, and says, "That's weird." The students' minds are racing as they ponder the subtle effects of the precise use of language, which is what makes this class so rewarding.

With the class engaged and animated, I offer another pair for them to work on in twos. This time, I ask them to tell me the difference between the following two sentences:

Their love blazed.

Their love burned.

Ashley, who is usually fairly quiet, speaks up: "The first one is like a high school love that is wild and out of control, like it's flared up. The second one is just constant." The class agrees, arriving at the conclusion that the first one seems out of control and short-lived, while the second seems to be a mellower love that might stand the test of time.

This is how we start working on literary analysis. Halfway through the first day, my students are articulating their analysis of diction. Once we have done several of these paired sentences, we move on to something more challenging.

Below is a paragraph taken from a classic piece of American literature, *Grapes of Wrath*, which I have altered. Working in pairs, the students' objective here is to highlight all the words that suggest deeper meaning.

> In the water-cut gullies the earth fluffed down to dry little streams. Gophers and ant lions started small rivers of fine sand. And as the soft sun shone day after day, the leaves of the young corn became less hardened and stiff; they curved at first, and then, as the central ribs of hardness grew softer, each leaf tilted downward. Then it was June, and the sun shone more clearly. The tanned lines on the corn leaves widened and blanketed the central ribs. The weeds receded in awe and parted, returning to their roots. The air was brisk and the sky more cottony-white; and every day the earth glimmered more from the fine, white sand.

Once the students have highlighted their passages, they list the words/phrases that they have chosen on a sheet of paper. I ask them to share the words with me, and I put them on the whiteboard. Here is a list that my class came up with this year:

Gullies	Softer	Cottony-white
Fluffed	Tilted	Glimmered
Streams	Clearly	Fine, white sand
Small rivers of fine sand	Tanned	
Soft sun	Blanketed	
Less hardened and stiff	Receded in awe	
Curved	Brisk	

At this stage, we talk about verbs because they often are the most important words in a sentence and writers choose them very carefully. The students share their verbs out loud while I write them on the board: *fluffed, curved, tilted, tanned, blanketed, receded in awe, glimmered.* In pairs, I have them discuss what feelings any of the words they chose evoke, then write out possible connotations for each of the words that they had previously listed.

At this point my class is truly analyzing literature, pulling apart how authors manipulate language for a desired effect. I love this moment when my students are truly reading with analytical eyes; Joanna is especially zealous, on a mission to hunt down those connotative words. She is sitting half out of her chair, her lanky frame bent over her desk as she shares her ideas with her partner. It is important during the early stages of analytical writing to include a great deal of discussion—students need to get very comfortable *saying* what they're thinking in collegiate terms before writing it out. The next step here is to talk about an overall feeling the author is creating through the manipulation of words. Joanna, all businesslike, shares her idea that the author creates a feeling of warmth and comfort in the passage. I ask why she thinks that, and which words in the passage led her to feel that way. Ashley jumps in, saying that the word *blanketed* has the connotation of security and safety. I love that we are in the first month of school, and already my students are on the first rung of the ladder that will lead to them succeeding in AP English classes. Joanna and Ashley's idea then becomes our thesis, and I write it on the board. Students are free to use it as their thesis or revise it or alter it if they want to.

Once I finish writing our thesis on the board, the class moves into the writing stage of analysis. As a class, they choose one word that supports our thesis: *fluffed.* Next, I ask what that word suggests or connotes. The responses center on a feeling of softness and comfort. So, I write on the board the first sentence of support in our paragraph. Here's our paragraph thus far:

The author creates a feeling of warmth and comfort in the passage. The narrator states that the "earth fluffed," which suggests a pleasant, soft sensation.

I have modeled a very basic analytical sentence that reflects what we have been talking about in our discussions of literature. There is not much that is new here, so my writers can safely attempt this step. I ask, "Do you think our readers will immediately follow our line of thinking, if our readers will get *why* 'earth fluffed' suggests a pleasant, soft sensation? Do we need some sort of bridge to lead from the analysis to the interpretation, from the text to the opinion we've formed about the text?" After a few minutes of discussion, it is decided that we do, and so we add a clause that I call a *bridge*.

> The author creates a feeling of warmth and comfort in the passage. The narrator states that the "earth fluffed," which suggests a pleasant, soft sensation, *as the word* fluffed *is usually associated with pillows, stuffed animals, furry cats, and other soothing objects.*

I have modeled a thesis, analysis, interpretation, and a bridge. At this stage, students have read and discussed the text, and seen a model of the writing, and now it is time to lead them through the writing. As I move around the room, I often ask students for permission to read really good lines out loud to the class, to further model successful writing. For the last five minutes of class, I put some of these on the ELMO and read through them, offering and asking for advice on revising them.

We constantly build in the Puente class, and I always have to remember to slow down the pace of analysis. My students have incredible potential this year, but if I simply clobber them over the head with a literary analysis writing assignment that asks too much right off the bat, I could lose some of them.

Reading Novels Analytically

As an English teacher, I know that there are plausible and implausible interpretations of literature, so teachers cannot permit an analytical free-for-all. There are wrong answers and illogical interpretations. Therefore, while we need to create safe environments for students to experiment with their own analyses and interpretations, we also need to shape their reading and writing skills until they can defend their insights in an articulate fashion.

When it comes to literary analysis, the preceding sentence serves as a sort of mission statement for me. I teach literature in a manner that accomplishes several goals:

1. to foster the love of reading quality literature and nonfiction
2. to enable students to use a variety of reading strategies in order to access quality literature and nonfiction
3. to create safe environments for experimentation with analysis and interpretation

I'd like to devote the next section of this chapter to the third goal: creating safe environments for experimentation with analysis and interpretation.

House on Mango Street

I cannot think of a better novel with which to begin teaching literary analysis to underrepresented students than Sandra Cisneros's *House on Mango Street*; however, the strategies that I use here can be applied to virtually any piece of quality literature. *House on Mango Street* appeals very strongly to my students. The novel centers on Esperanza, a young Latina who struggles against the culture of poverty in hopes of obtaining a better life one day and returning to improve her neighborhood. In my class, after we write the birth order paper and I introduce students to literary analysis, we begin reading Cisneros's work, and set the tone for what I hope will be a life-changing English class.

It's a Monday in late September, and today my Puente class will begin the novel. I put the first paragraph of the novel up on the ELMO for my students to read:

> We didn't always live on Mango Street. Before that we lived on Loomis on the third floor, and before that we lived on Keeler. Before Keeler it was Paulina, and before that I can't remember. But what I remember most is moving a lot. Each time it seemed there'd be one more of us. By the time we got to Mango Street we were six—Mama, Papa, Carlos, Kiki, my sister Nenny and me.

Continuing with the same analytical approach to literature that we've been using recently, I ask my students to highlight words or phrases that offer insights to this family—what conclusions can we come to based on what the speaker says here?

As they start sharing their opinions with me, I follow each statement with a question along the lines of "How do you know that?" or "Why do you think that?" I try to reinforce the connection that writers must make between their analysis (the textual piece that leads to insight) and interpretation (the writer's opinion about the textual piece). After some discussion, my students arrive at five basic conclusions:

- The family is not wealthy, evidenced by the fact that they live on the third floor and probably don't own a home.
- The family is not too stable, evidenced by the fact that they move around so much (more than four places mentioned here).
- The brother and the speaker are probably not very close since he's the only one without a nickname.
- The family is large (6 people).
- The speaker sounds like a young kid.

We now read the first vignette of the book together. I ask students to highlight words/phrases/lines that the author possibly uses for effect, and then we share those highlighted pieces of text. Images such as the "tight steps" mentioned later in the text are among those highlighted; Estephanie interprets that to mean that the narrator feels closed in by the smallness of Mango Street. We continue sharing highlighted phrases and then offering possible interpretations of them. At this stage of the analysis process, we're just taking in information and offering possibilities or creating theories. Eventually, we will test those theories, but for now, all student comments are welcome. Too often, students are led to believe that we teachers get the text immediately—because we make them think that we do. They don't see all the time spent in advance considering possibilities, listening to and reading other interpretations, and sometimes even letting the teacher's edition do the work for us. Students who don't see themselves as college material (yet) need to feel safe in a situation like this. For most underrepresented students, simply becoming comfortable sharing their ideas is a major victory, and is a goal that should be encouraged rather than squelched.

Therefore, when they read through *House on Mango Street*, I try to create lots of opportunities for interpretation without penalty. My writers create an analytical reading log that they add to as they read. They copy a passage from the text and note the page number in the first column, then write questions and possible outcomes in the second and third columns. Figure 3.1 is an example that I give them that shows the format and content I'm looking for.

Figure 3.1 Sample Analytical Reading Log

Text	Questions	Possible Outcomes
"This was the house Papa talked about when he held up a lottery ticket and . . . Mama dreamed up in the stories she told us before we went to bed." (4)	Do the narrator's parents truly expect to one day own a really nice house or are they just keeping up the pretense for the sake of the children? Why are her parents poor? Are they lazy poor or hardworking poor? Does the narrator see the parents' dreams with insight or does she truly believe what her parents say?	The family will end up in a nice house by the end of the book. The narrator will run away to live somewhere that is more like the dream house of her parents. The family will end up happy with their neighborhood even though it's in a ghetto.
"For the time being, Mama says. Temporary, says Papa. But I know how those things go." (5)	Do the parents have a plan to get a nicer house? What does Esperanza think of her parents?	This book will be more about the narrator's family than about the house. The house is a symbol for something else. The narrator and her family will get in a fight over the house.

I want my students to ask questions and consider various possibilities here; it doesn't matter if they're right or not. As they read, I have them complete log entries showing their analysis. When a reading assignment is due, students share these logs in small groups and we discuss them as a class. The question I very quickly begin inserting into the discussion of each vignette is "What was the author's purpose in this chapter?" I work with their verbal responses until they sound appropriately collegiate and are expressed in language worthy of an AP English writer.

As we quickly progress through the book, we start piecing vignettes together and look for themes running through Cisneros's writing. *House on Mango*

Street touches on so many issues that underrepresented students face every day that the discussions are usually rich and engaging for the students, and fascinating for me. Some of the issues that this year's class has pulled out of the novel include the role of women in poor neighborhoods, immigration and assimilation, poverty, education, the combination of race and income, growing up, childhood fears, social injustice, and the interaction between the individual and the community—topics that will be brought up consistently throughout the two years I have with my Puente students. I want to emphasize here that I don't bring up any of these topics—the students do. My job is to facilitate their analysis and interpretation, and to foster a new skill for them: synthesis (piecing together the separate elements of their analysis into a coherent whole).

This year it took me about three weeks to have the students read the book (after the first chapter, all reading is done outside of class); we continued the reading logs and class discussions during that time, and practiced our literary analysis skills in mini-lessons and in the writer's notebook, where my students write five pages of literary analysis a week just for practice.

As we read the book, students are given their writing prompt, which is as follows:

> Consider Sandra Cisneros's *The House on Mango Street* and the various themes that she presents, and choose one for discussion in your paper. In a well-constructed, thoughtful essay, analyze the details that display the theme you choose. Be sure to pull support from several vignettes (select from four or more for stronger development).
>
> Your essay should also reflect sophisticated and varied sentence structure and display both a mature vocabulary and a mastery of the conventions of the English language. Obviously, you'll want to pay close attention to using the skills we've covered recently.

Students immediately begin working on their theses, taking into account the work they did in the analytical reading logs and their writer's notebooks. The next day, we go around the room sharing our theses—I'll sometimes offer advice, and much revision takes place during this time of sharing. At this stage, I ask them not to write anything else in their introduction other than the thesis; we'll return to the introductions when we finish with the body (more on that later).

Reviewing the writing process, I have my writers, after composing their theses, begin pulling evidence from the text (analysis) and their view of what each piece reveals (interpretation). All their combinations of analysis and interpretation must work together (synthesis) to support the thesis. The format is simple; students simply draw a line down a sheet of paper and put the analysis with the page number on the left, the interpretation on the right. A sample is shown in Figure 3.2.

Figure 3.2 Prewriting Sample

Thesis: In Sandra Cisneros's *The House on Mango Street*, she illustrates the despair and desperation felt by many inhabitants of the barrio. However, even amidst the squalor of an impoverished neighborhood, Cisneros highlights a few glimmers of hope for those who look carefully.

"small . . . with tight steps" small windows, crumbling bricks, swollen front door (4)	Mango Street is full of poverty and suppression—first statements of book
" . . . they'll just have to move a little farther north from Mango Street, a little farther away every time people like us keep moving in" (13)	Implies that undesirable people (like Esperanza) are moving into Mango Street, and those that can, are moving out.
"Marin . . . is waiting for a car to stop, a star to fall, someone to change her life" (27)	Common approach—hope for someone else to rescue a character from poverty
"she says she's just visiting and next weekend her husband's going to take her home. But the weekends come and go and Ruthie stays" (69)	Illusory hope of relying on someone else to rescue
"and always there is someone offering sweeter drinks, someone promising to keep them on a silver string" (80)	Reinforces the illusory hope of relying on others
"She says she is in love, but I think she did it to escape" (101)	Illustration of someone who relied on someone else to be rescued, but in the end becomes just as trapped as before

"...I am a red balloon, a balloon tied to an anchor" (9)	Esperanza is held back by Mango Street
"when she is holding you, holding you and you feel safe, is the warm smell of bread before you bake it" (6)	Family brings safety and hope
"it's like drops of water" (20)	Relief against backdrop of despair
"four who grew despite concrete. Four who reach and do not forget to reach." (75)	Shows that despite obstacles, some can make it out of poverty

After completing their prewriting, students begin drafting their paper. Again, the only thing I want in their introductions right now is a thesis. During the drafting process, which takes a couple of days, students are exposed to mini-lessons on scope, unity, using specific examples, using transitions, using academic language, and comma usage. When I feel that their papers are as thoroughly supported, logically arranged, articulately worded, and closely edited as possible (the entire process takes about three weeks), I return to the introduction and we focus on that as a class.

Writing Leads

Once I'm comfortable with the quality of the support in their essays, I introduce the concept of LEADS, which I've based on a strategy shared with me by Nina Woolridge, co-chair of the South Basin Writing Project in Southern California. Figure 3.3 illustrates how LEADS works.

LEADS is a step above the common "hook" taught in elementary and junior high schools. I've had way too many papers presented to me, even at the college level, that begin with some inane question like "Have you ever been to jail?" or "Have you ever had an abortion?" Those yes/no questions completely fail to hook anyone if the reader's response is "no." The LEADS strategy is a little different; some might complain that it is a bit formulaic, but introduced at the beginning of ninth grade, it gives fledgling writers a starting point to work with that they will grow out of before they are done with my class.

Figure 3.3 LEADS

L	E	A	D	S
Leading Question *What is the source of evil?*	**Eminent Quotation (universal)** *"The belief in a supernatural source of evil is not necessary; men alone are quite capable of every wickedness."*	**Anecdote** *When I was little, my parents took my brothers, sisters and me to Disneyland for the best day of my life. The only one left behind was my beloved, well-behaved dog. After a day of fun and enjoyment, we returned home to an unpleasant surprise: my dog had completely torn apart my dad's favorite chair.*	**Direct, Startling Statement** *The only thing keeping human civilization from dropping off into complete evil are a few, frail laws.*	**Story in the News** *Four million dollars. That seems to be the going rate for the freedom to flout laws, morals, and civilized behavior. Sounds outrageous? Just ask Kobe Bryant.*
Answer the Question *As much as we look to external causes for evil acts – following orders, poverty, or a bad home life – evil resides deep in the hearts of all of us.*	**Reflect on the Quotation** *This statement from Joseph Conrad communicates the truth that the source of evil is not external, but rather dwells in every person.*	**Explain the Anecdote** *Humans, it seems, are much the same. When left to our own devices, and free from authority, we, too, will commit horrendous acts against others. Evil is instinctive.*	**Expand on the Statement** *Yet, we continue to spin happily along, oblivious to the fact that all that is good and just in our society could be easily dashed aside by a few people pursuing their true nature.*	**Highlight the Themes** *Four million dollars, of course, was the price paid for his wife's ring to placate her after his adultery. Apparently, once you achieve his fame and fortune, a sense of being above societal restrictions develops. In his defense, he did what probably would come naturally to any of us freed from society's restraints . . . allow the inherent evil to determine behavior.*

Connect the LEAD to the thesis: In Sir William Golding's *Lord of the Flies*, he illustrates this idea.

Thesis

The characters and their actions indicate a sad yet truthful aspect of humanity: just below the surface, all of us have an evil streak in our soul that resists the restraints of civilization.

There are four steps when using LEADS: engage, expand, connect, and finally, state the thesis. At the top of the page, students will choose a strategy that will engage the reader, and write an engaging lead in the top section. Below that, they expand on that engaging beginning in a way that nudges the reader closer to the thesis. Next, they connect the lead to the thesis. Finally, they state the thesis. Each step can have as many sentences as it needs. As writers move on, they quickly develop other strategies than the ones listed, and they begin to play with building up to a thesis and presenting it later in their paper. At this stage, however, they follow the structure. I give them a handout of Figure 3.3, which gets placed in the writer's notebook.

Here's what a sample introduction would look like, then, that followed the eminent quotation strategy:

> "The belief in a supernatural source of evil is not necessary; men alone are quite capable of every wickedness." This statement from Joseph Conrad communicates the truth that the source of evil is not external, but rather dwells in every person. Sir William Golding illustrates this idea in his *Lord of the Flies*. The characters and their actions indicate a sad yet truthful aspect of humanity: just below the surface, all of us have an evil streak in our soul that resists the restraints of civilization.

When asked what the most difficult aspect of writing is, most students will reply "the introduction" or "the beginning." Therefore, in my class, we usually wait until the end of the paper to write the introduction. In a sense, it is easier to introduce something that is already written than something that has yet to take shape. Also, most students feel they need to write for a little bit before they really get into their groove; if that's true, it makes more sense to write the most challenging part of a paper after they've already been writing for a bit.

I've learned that when working with underrepresented students, I often have to work through each element of writing methodically and purposefully. In my earlier days as a teacher, I would often simply assign the paper and have thirty-odd sets of mediocrity and disappointment handed in. I've experienced greater success actually showing them what it is I wish them to do, then teaching each section of the paper as they go through the writing process.

However, by this stage, the students are ready to turn in their first literary analysis paper. At the end of this chapter, I've included a sample of a final draft of this paper.

Literary Analysis Timed Writing

Now that the students have gone through a process paper analyzing literature, I intend to give them a few opportunities at analytical timed writing assignments. In my Puente class, we take the best five timed writing scores in a semester and drop the rest, so ideally the students aren't feeling quite as nervous as they would be otherwise. For the first analytical timed writing, I have chosen a poem, "Cincinnati."

It is now December. We are reading Elie Wiesel's *Night,* and the class is very interested in World War II. After reading a couple of poems to practice analyzing out loud, I hand them the text of "Cincinnati":

Cincinnati

BY MITSUYE YAMADA

Freedom at last
in this town aimless
I walked against the rush
hour traffic
My first day
in a real city
where
no one knew me.
No one except one
hissing voice that said
dirty jap
warm spittle on my right cheek.
I turned and faced
the shop window
and my spittled face
spilled onto a hill
of books.
Words on display.
In Government Square
people criss-crossed
the street

like the spokes of
a giant wheel.
I lifted my right hand
but it would not obey me.
My other hand fumbled for a hankie.
My tears would not
wash it. They stopped
and parted.
My hankie brushed
the forked
tears and spittle
together.
I edged toward the curb
loosened my fisthold
and the bleached laced
mother-ironed hankie blossomed in
the gutter atop teeth marked
gum wads and heeled candy wrappers.
Everyone knew me.
(1998)

The students are instructed to highlight anything that stands out to them, even
if they can't figure out exactly why. They are also asked to underline anything
that they question, either for clarification or to offer a possible interpretation.
Here is the conversation that my Puente class had regarding the poem:

CARLOS: What is "dirty jap"? Is that like a dirty Japanese person?

ESTEFANIE: That's what I thought. What about "warm spittle?" Is it spit?

JOANNA: Yeah, it's spit on his face.

CHRIS: Who is the "hissing voice"? I know it's the person saying "dirty jap"
but who is it?

TURNER: That's a good question . . . Anyone have any thoughts on this?

CHRIS: [answering his own question] It says "no one knew him," so it's just some guy in the street? [class responds, murmuring "yes"]

JOANNA: I don't get this—what are "spokes"?

JOE: They're like metal . . . little sticks on a wheel.

TURNER: Can you imagine that now, the streets like spokes?

JOANNA: Yeah.

DANNY: What does "my right hand would not obey me" mean?

ALVARO: He couldn't move it . . . He was paralyzed.

ESTEFANIE: What does it mean that his "hankie blossomed in . . ." Oh wait, I get it now. His hankie fell, right?

DANNY: I don't get why it says "no one knew me" and then "everyone knew me."

ESTEPHANIE: I think everyone knew he was Japanese.

EDGAR: Everyone knew he was Asian but they didn't know his personality.

JOE: Everyone knew he was Japanese, yeah.

EDGAR: It doesn't matter what his personality was like, just that he's Asian. People only see what they want to see. They didn't want to see his personality, just that he's Asian.

ESTEPHANIE: OK, but wait. I thought this was a girl because of the hankie. Is it a boy or a girl?

JOE: You can't spit at a little kid. It can't be a little kid.

CARLOS: You wouldn't spit at a woman, either. I think it's a man.

I love class discussions like this. My role is appropriately small, and the students are truly analyzing the text. However, it doesn't just happen automatically; these freshmen have almost been programmed after having read *The House on Mango Street* to pull out text details in order to formulate interpretations. At this stage of the game, December of the freshman year, I'm not too concerned with misinterpretation: the freedom to bounce their ideas off one another will take care of most of that.

I am beaming at the conclusion of the discussion; my students have clarified difficult passages, reasoned through some of the subtleties in the text, focused on the central theme, and discussed key passages without much direction from me. I now give them a deliberately incomplete model I wrote of a literary analysis piece on the poem, shown in Figure 3.4. We talk through the elements of what the piece does well.

Figure 3.4 Model Draft of a Literary Analysis Paper

In the poem "Cincinnati," Mitsuye Yamada expresses his view that the Japanese-Americans imprisoned during World War II suffered hardship even after being released.	Intro begins with just the thesis; identifies genre and title, communicates the thesis of the essay.
The poem opens with a deceptively celebratory tone, as the speaker achieves "freedom at last." However, he follows this statement with describing his first moments of freedom as "aimless" and walking "against the rush-hour traffic," signaling the opposition he is about to face in this town. Just as he physically is pressing against the tide of people, so too will he be overwhelmed by the weight of their prejudice. At this point in the poem, though, he feels completely anonymous and unnoticed, as he proclaims that "no one knew" him. The statement is partly true: no one knew his character, his morals, his person. No one knows what makes him an individual, and as the poem progresses, the reader is led to see that people in the town only know him for his physical characteristics.	Textual Evidence / Commentary is blended throughout Bridge Ties in to thesis
In fact, his first encounter is with a "hissing voice," emphasizing the evil of the character by using a word associated with a snake, the original embodiment of sin. With this phrase, the reader is led to react against those who looked down on Japanese-Americans. The voice calls him a "dirty jap," again aligning the reader against the Cincinnati native because of the offensive nature of the word	Transition integrated concrete detail, quoted only words that matter Focusing on effect on the reader

At this stage, students are asked to go through a prewriting activity: pulling apart the text and focusing on (1) the effect of each piece of text on the reader, and (2) how it contributes to a possible theme/thesis. It is a process similar to our approach to *The House on Mango Street* and is one step closer to timed writings with cold texts, which will be necessary for both the California High School Exit Exam and for Advanced Placement tests.

Here is the first analytical timed writing that my students take:

TIMED WRITING

World War II permeated nearly every culture and sub-culture on the globe. From Polish prisoners of war to Japanese citizens in the United States, people everywhere were forced to examine their belief systems, their view of government, and even their ethnicity.

DIRECTIONS:

Read the poem "Cincinnati." Then, in a well-constructed, thoughtful essay, argue what you think the "big idea," or the *theme* of this poem is. Use textual evidence as support for your views, just like you did for the *Mango Street* paper.

Your essay should also reflect a sophisticated and varied sentence structure and display a mature vocabulary as well as a mastery of the conventions of the English language. *Please double-space your essay* and write in dark ink.

For the second literary analysis timed writing, I take the altered passage from John Steinbeck's *Grapes of Wrath* that I discussed on page 39 and pair it with the original version. The prior analysis helps put students into a confident mind-set, and the analysis of the original version (which they have never seen before) is usually quite strong as well. Having so many supports—prior analysis, multiple practice sessions, dropping the lower scores—helps to reduce the fear that underrepresented students often feel in testing environments like this. At the same time, they are, in a sense, analyzing a cold text because they have never seen Passage 2 before. For underrepresented students, the path to success in AP courses has a gradual incline throughout ninth and tenth grade, and as we continue working through analytical timed writings, the students stand increasingly on their own and need less and less help from me.

PRE-AP PRACTICE TW

Read the following two passages describing United States farmland. Then, write an essay in which you analyze how the use of language in each passage reveals the purpose of its writer.

Passage 1

In the water-cut gullies the earth fluffed down in dry little streams. Gophers and ant lions started small rivers of fine sand. And as the soft sun shone day after day, the leaves of the young corn became less hardened and stiff; they curved at first, and then, as the central ribs of hardness grew softer, each leaf tilted downward. Then it was June, and the sun shone more clearly. The tanned lines on the corn leaves widened and blanketed the central ribs. The weeds receded in awe and parted, returning to their roots. The air was brisk and the sky more cottony-white; and every day the earth glimmered more from the fine, white sand.

Passage 2

In the water-cut gullies the earth dusted down in dry little streams. Gophers and ant lions started small avalanches. And as the sharp sun struck day after day, the leaves of the young corn became less stiff and erect; they bent in a curve at first, and then, as the central ribs of strength grew weak, each leaf tilted downward. Then it was June, and the sun shone more fiercely. The brown lines on the corn leaves widened and moved in on the central ribs. The weeds frayed and edged back toward their roots. The air was thin and the sky more pale; and every day the earth paled.

Effective Verbs

I might be bordering on obsession here, but I have this thing for verbs. Such a small task, to upgrade a weak verb, yet what a difference it makes. It's like switching your favorite TV program to high definition. Maybe I *am* obsessed, but one of the ways to get students to analyze quality writing is to have them pay close attention to their own writing. So, as we approach further literary analysis, I introduce the concept of using effective verbs. The weak verbs— *be, being, been, is, am, was, were*—should be used sparingly. I ask students to write one analytical paragraph and then highlight all the verbs: weak verbs in yellow, effective verbs in blue, all other verbs in green. At a glance, students can see the nature of their verb usage (generally speaking, the more weak verbs they use, the weaker their writing is in terms of craft). Then, we set about upgrading the verbs and moving their paragraphs along faster (replacing weak verbs tends to speed up the flow of the paragraph).

In literary analysis, there is a tendency to overuse the word *shows*. Below are the verbs that I suggest using in place of this word. Students place the list in their writer's notebook; when they choose to use a word they are unfamiliar with, they are encouraged to check with me to ensure they are using it properly.

EFFECTIVE VERBS FOR *SHOWS*

Follow-up Opportunities for Literary Analysis

Conveys	Presents	Creates
Reveals	Implements	Permeates
Connotes	Enhances	Flows
Delineates	Contrasts	Illustrates
Emphasizes	Demonstrates	Paints
Accomplishes	Reflects	Displays
Advocates	Exemplifies	Portrays
Alludes to	Amplifies	Spotlights
Suggests	Juxtaposes	
Highlights	Asserts	
Represents	Contributes	

Once I've completed the first paper, I move on to another genre of writing for a while. Students resume writing five pages per week in their writer's notebook, and I ask them to vary their discourse patterns to include both expository and analysis pieces so that they're refining the skills we've gone over. From time to time, I will return to literary analysis for shorter pieces and timed writings. One piece in particular that I love using during the freshman year is an excerpt from Charles Dickens's *Hard Times*, specifically, the beginning of Chapter Five. This is what Dickens writes:

Coketown, to which Messrs. Bounderby and Gradgrind now walked, was a triumph of fact; it had no greater taint of fancy in it than Mrs Gradgrind herself. Let us strike the key-note, Coketown, before pursuing our tune.

It was a town of red brick, or of brick that would have been red if the smoke and ashes had allowed it; but as matters stood, it was a town of unnatural red and black like the painted face of a savage. It was a town of machinery and tall chimneys, out of which interminable serpents of smoke trailed themselves for ever and ever, and never got uncoiled.

It had a black canal in it, and a river that ran purple with ill-smelling dye, and vast piles of building full of windows where there was a rattling and a trembling all day long, and where the piston of the steam-engine worked monotonously up and down, like the head of an elephant in a state of melancholy madness. It contained several large streets all very like one another, and many small streets still more like one another, inhabited by people equally like one another, who all went in and out at the same hours, with the same sound upon the same pavements, to do the same work, and to whom every day was the same as yesterday and to-morrow, and every year the counterpart of the last and the next.

These attributes of Coketown were in the main inseparable from the work by which it was sustained; against them were to be set off, comforts of life which found their way all over the world, and elegancies of life which made, we will not ask how much of the fine lady, who could scarcely bear to hear the place mentioned. The rest of its features were voluntary, and they were these.

You saw nothing in Coketown but what was severely workful. If the members of a religious persuasion built a chapel there—as the members of eighteen religious persuasions had done—they made it a pious warehouse of red brick, with sometimes (but this is only in highly ornamented examples) a bell in a birdcage on the top of it. The solitary exception was the New Church; a stuccoed edifice with a square steeple over the door, terminating in four short pinnacles like florid wooden legs. All the public inscriptions in the town were painted alike, in severe characters of black and white. The jail might have been the infirmary, the infirmary might have been the jail, the town-hall might have been either, or both, or anything else, for anything that appeared to the contrary in the graces of their construction. Fact, fact, fact, everywhere in the material aspect of the town; fact, fact, fact, everywhere in the immaterial. The M'Choakumchild school was all fact, and the school of design was all fact, and the relations between master and man were all fact, and everything was fact

57

between the lying-in hospital and the cemetery, and what you couldn't state in figures, or show to be purchasable in the cheapest market and salable in the dearest, was not, and never should be, world without end, Amen.

As with prior analysis, students examine the words and details, highlighting whatever stands out to them. With this piece, however, after considering the diction, I have students focus a bit more on *syntax*, or sentence structure. As usual, they are in pairs or groups of three, discussing the passage before sharing their results with the class. They make a T-chart detailing their analysis and interpretation.

Fairly quickly, my students pick up on the ugliness and dirt that permeate this passage ("smoke," "ashes," "unnatural red," "savage," all from the second paragraph alone). Edgar identifies the emphasis on monotony in the fourth paragraph, and once he states this observation, I have the students take a second look at the syntax and ask them what they notice. Maggie notices that "there are only two sentences in the paragraph, and they're both real long."

I ask the class to reread the second sentence: "It contained several large streets all very like one another, and many small streets still more like one another, inhabited by people equally like one another, who all went in and out at the same hours, with the same sound upon the same pavements, to do the same work, and to whom every day was the same as yesterday and to-morrow, and every year the counterpart of the last and the next." Ozzy states that the sentence goes on and on, and correctly notes how frustrating it is because it never really goes anywhere. I respond, "What is the author's purpose in writing the sentence this way? After all, Dickens was an accomplished writer in his time; did this convoluted sentence come about because of a lack of skill?"

Johanna replies that the sentence is written in a way that is like Coketown itself, "all confusing." In short, the syntax mirrors the frustrating monotony discussed in the sentence.

My students are in ninth grade and they have reached a new level of literary analysis: the examination of syntax (consider the sentence structure of the very last sentence in this text). Everything we read for this class, whether we are writing literary analysis or not, will at some point be examined for wording and for sentence structure, or for *diction* and *syntax*. Throughout the process, I am consciously grooming my students for AP English classes, and I am conscious of the fact that I have the rest of their freshman year and all of their sophomore year to get them prepared for that class; I am constantly aware that success in AP classes opens many doors for my students, and increases the odds of their succeeding at a university.

I need to emphasize that I am opposed to teaching my students an artificial construct in order to get a passing score on a test. By slowly building *authentic* literary analysis skills, my writers become closer readers and more detailed writers, both of which are skills essential for the university and for life beyond it.

Notating the Text

In September of my writers' sophomore year, we read William Golding's *Lord of the Flies*. The book is rich with lush imagery, connotative diction, and syntactical moves for students to pull apart. Consider the beginning of Chapter Three:

> Jack was bent double. He was down like a sprinter, his nose only a few inches from the humid earth. The tree trunks and the creepers that festooned them lost themselves in a green dusk thirty feet above him, and all about was the undergrowth. There was only the faintest indication of a trail here; a cracked twig and what might be the impression of one side of a hoof. He lowered his chin and stared at the traces as though he would force them to speak to him. Then dog-like, uncomfortably on all fours yet unheeding his discomfort, he stole forward five yards and stopped. Here was loop of creeper with a tendril pendant from a node. The tendril was polished on the underside; pigs, passing through the loop, brushed it with their bristly hide.
>
> Jack crouched with his face a few inches away from this clue, then started forward into the semi-darkness of the undergrowth. His sandy hair, considerably longer than it had been when they dropped in, was lighter now; and his bare back was a mass of dark freckles and peeling sunburn. A sharpened stick about five feet long trailed from his right hand, and except for a pair of tattered shorts held up by his knife-belt he was naked. He closed his eyes, raised his head and breathed in gently with flared nostrils, assessing the current of warm air for information. The forest and he were very still.

At length he let out his breath in a long sigh and opened his eyes. They were bright blue, eyes that in this frustration seemed bolting and nearly mad. He passed his tongue across dry lips and scanned the uncommunicative forest. Then again he stole forward and cast this way and that over the ground.

The silence of the forest was more oppressive than the heat, and at this hour of the day there was not even the whine of insects. Only when Jack himself roused a gaudy bird from a primitive nest of sticks was the silence shattered and echoes set ringing by a harsh cry that seemed to come out of the abyss of ages. Jack himself shrank at this cry with a hiss of indrawn breath, and for a minute became less a hunter than a furtive thing, ape-like among the tangle of trees. Then the trail, the frustration, claimed him again and he searched the ground avidly. By the trunk of a vast tree that grew pale flowers on its grey bark he checked, closed his eyes, and once more drew in the warm air; and this time his breath came short, there was even a passing pallor in his face, and then the surge of blood again. He passed like a shadow under the darkness of the tree and crouched, looking down at the trodden ground at his feet.

After having read the text on their own, students revisit it with a pen or pencil, a common occurrence in my class. The first thing I have them do is to circle or underline words, phrases, images, or syntactical elements that stand out to them. Then, they share these with a partner or in groups of three, marking up the text further based on what they hear from their partners. Once this is done, they begin looking for connections between their notes; in other words, can they discern the author's purpose? Once they have a theory regarding the author's purpose, I might draw them back to specifics in the text, or push them to reword their opinion or to look for additional support for their view. When each pair/small group has come up with some opinion regarding Golding's purpose here, we discuss the passage so that everyone has a working thesis regarding the text. Then, I send them back to the text again, asking what else they can add that could be seen as reinforcing the author's purpose here. After a few minutes, every copy of the passage in the room should be somehow marked up.

The next stage is for students to begin jotting down quick comments that nail down their interpretations. For instance, "bent double" and "down like a sprinter" indicates that Jack did not stand upright and therefore suggests that his gait was more animal than human. Later, the narrator refers to Jack as "dog-like" and "ape-like," reinforcing this animalistic description of Jack. On my writers' papers, they would have circled or underlined "bent double" and "down like a sprinter" and written "like an animal"; in the margins next to the circled or underlined "doglike" and "apelike," they would write "animal" each time.

We spend much time with partners working through the text, notating what we've already spotted. My students discuss their views with their partners as they work through the text, and as I move quickly about the room, I look for lots of writing on their pages.

When I feel comfortable with the amount of notating, I take an unmarked passage and put it on the ELMO, and we walk through the text, one line at a time, with students volunteering their observations. I note everything the students say, and ask them to try to add to their observations based on what they hear from the other groups. At this stage, every paper is heavily marked up.

We repeat this process with several other passages throughout the novel—the passage where they kill the pig in Chapter Eight is especially rich in imagery, although perhaps a bit too graphic for some tastes—until I feel comfortable that my students are marking up the text like English majors.

Zooming In, Integrating Quotations, and Blending Analysis and Interpretation

In November and December of the sophomore year, we read Ray Bradbury's *Fahrenheit 451*, my favorite book to teach. At this stage of their development, my students understand how to approach literary analysis and formulate their views; with this text, we work on the issues of craft that are particular to this genre of writing.

First, here is the text that we work with:

Part One: In the passage below, consider how Bradbury uses literary devices (imagery, diction/connotation, syntax, metaphor/simile) in order to achieve an effect. Highlight, circle, or mark up the text as you read and reread the passage.

He opened the bedroom door.

It was like coming into the cold marbled room of a mausoleum after the moon has set. Complete darkness, not a hint of the silver world outside, the windows tightly shut, the chamber a tomb world where no sound from the great city would penetrate. The room was not empty.

He listened.

The little mosquito-delicate dancing hum in the air, the electrical murmur of a hidden wasp snug in its special pink warm nest. The music was almost loud enough so he could follow the tune.

He felt his smile slide away, melt, fold, over and down on itself like a tallow skin, like the stuff of a fantastic candle burning too long and now collapsing and now blown out. Darkness. He was not happy. He was not happy. He said the words to himself. He recognized this as the true state of affairs. He wore his happiness like a mask and the girl had run off across the lawn with the mask and there was no way of going to knock on her door and ask for it back.

Once we've marked up the text, drafted our essays, responded to each other's content, and engaged in surface revision, we are ready to examine the craft of our papers. Although many of my students have picked up some of these strategies, this is the stage when I make sure all my writers are following the conventions of literary analysis.

I begin with what I call "zooming in." Simply put, my students start out in ninth grade plopping an entire quoted sentence all by itself onto their paper, followed by an entire sentence of explanation. Zooming in is simply quoting only the important stuff. For instance, in the first paragraph above, "It was like coming into the cold marbled room of a mausoleum after the moon has set" is a key line. Unfortunately, students will often quote the entire thing rather than zooming in on the worthwhile elements—*cold marbled, mausoleum, after the moon has set*—and just quoting those words/phrases. Having students go back and underline only the essential words/phrases of a line helps them trim the extraneous words from their argument.

After zooming in, we work on integrating the much-smaller quotations into our own sentences: *Bradbury paints a picture of a "cold marbled room of a mausoleum."* We've taken the essential parts of the original text and worked it into our own sentence. The next step is to look at our notations and decide what interpretation should follow this information. When we've done that, we're ready for the next phase, which is blending our analysis and interpretation.

Basically, we're going to take the sentence with the quoted text and blend it with our own ideas: *Bradbury paints a picture of a "cold marbled room of a mausoleum," suggesting that since their bedroom resembles a house of death, their love likewise has expired.* Keep in mind that students have already notated their way through the text, so all we're doing here is playing with craft. By the time this short essay is finished, many of my writers produce work that indicates that they will probably go on to succeed in AP English classes.

Other Approaches to Literary Analysis and Other Texts

I realize that there might be a bit of controversy stemming from this particular chapter; some might contend that I focus too much on the AP exam and allow it to control too much of my curriculum. In my defense, I do have students write other pieces of literary analysis—Elie Wiesel's experiences as they relate to Maslow's Hierarchy of Needs, tactics used by the pigs in *Animal Farm* and how they compare to today's advertising strategies, issues reflected in *Lord of the Flies*, and the effects of biculturality in *Bless Me Ultima*, for instance— but this is a book about getting historically underrepresented students into universities with the skills necessary to succeed. Although micro-analysis enables students to identify the manipulation of language for a desired effect, a definite asset in today's world of talk radio and 24-hour news stations, the type of micro-analysis we do in my class also enables my students to succeed in later AP classes and in college. Further, many prestigious universities pay close attention to the rigor of the courses that students have taken; AP classes increase student access to these universities. If, in regular English classes, we fail to expose students to the writing demands of college, we are complicit in the closing of opportunities that we ought to be fighting to grant these students. In short, if we teachers of underrepresented students don't increase the number of students gaining access to rigorous AP classes and the International Baccalaureate curriculum, then the dreams of many of our students will continue to go unrealized.

Sample Paper—*House on Mango Street*

MILDRED LIMA
PUENTE ENGLISH
PERIOD ONE
MR. TURNER

Ralph Waldo Emerson once stated, "People only see what they are prepared to see." Sandra Cisneros illustrates this idea in her book, *The House on Mango Street* by showing numerous characters living on Mango Street who would rather be content with their unfulfilling lives than want to see beyond Mango Street, thus a better future. Cisneros reveals that living in a predominately poor Latino neighborhood begins to affect the thinking of its inhabitants, who then have a difficult time figuring out their identity in this neighborhood and in the U.S. itself.

Esperanza, the central character, states in the vignette, "Those Who Don't," "all brown all around we're safe," demonstrating a Latina's way of thinking about the world. More specifically, like most Latinas, Esperanza is not as concerned with staying out of harm's way, as she is with being protected from the judgment of others outside her world. In brief, Esperanza fears judgment more than physical danger. This idea is supported by Cathy, a minor character, when she states, "they'll just have to move . . . a little farther away every time people like us keep moving in." This scene indicates that the white, more prosperous people will keep moving out, while the poor Latinos keep moving in. Both events illustrate that Esperanza identifies herself and her community in a negative light.

Afterward in the same vignette, Esperanza states, "but watch us drive into a neighborhood of another color and our knees go shakity shake and our car windows get rolled up tight and our eyes look straight." This statement shows that Latinos, similar to Esperanza, shy away from a different culture because they can't identify themselves with a different race. Cisneros shows that Latinos, who aren't with their people often feel too intimidated to show their full potential due to the fear of being judged and belittled; further; Cisneros shows that Latinos feel indifferent outside their own race.

In the vignette, "Bums in the Attic," Esperanza displays hopelessness when she states, "I am tired of looking at what we can't have. When we win the lottery Mama begins, and then I stop listening." Cisneros draws attention to the obvious gap between the two social classes making Esperanza feel ashamed. As Cisneros demonstrates Esperanza's feelings, it further shows that Latinos feel pity for themselves and take no action other than hope.

In a later vignette, Esperanza describes Geraldo, another minor character, as "just another brazer who didn't speak English. Just another wetback. The ones who always look ashamed." Esperanza calls one of her own a "wetback," thus confirming how derogatory Latinos look at one another. The concept of Latino versus Latino that Cisneros demonstrates shows the lack of progression in the Latino culture.

Equally important is the experience and perspective of others living on Mango Street. Rafaela who is "still young but getting old," and "gets locked indoors because her husband is afraid Rafaela will run away." Esperanza absorbs Rafaela's hunger for life, similar to another of Esperanza's neighbors, Minerva, "who is always mad like a house on fire— always something wrong. She has many troubles . . ." Neither Minerva nor Rafaela are fully satisfied with their lives on Mango Street; thus they are unable to make themselves stand out in Mango Street. Esperanza recognizes how her neighbors crumble as they yearn for one goal: a satisfying life. Regardless, Esperanza, like her neighbors, are unable to define themselves in Mango Street.

Similarly, Esperanza states, "I am a red balloon, a balloon tied to an anchor." That phrase specifies that she, like everyone else, feels held back by Mango Street and unable to escape, still hoping one day she will be released and be able to soar. This line, the heart of the book, expresses built-up frustrations over time—the anchor is Mango Street, and the red balloon is Esperanza, struggling to be set free.

In the midst of all the despair presented in *The House on Mango Street,* Cisneros offers a glimmer of hope. Aunt Lupe provides Esperanza with encouraging words, "you must keep writing it will set you free," showing that there is light at the end of the tunnel. In brief, if there is will, determination, and hope, anything is possible, which many living in Mango Street may have forgotten due to the negative prospects they have in life. After Aunt Lupe gives these motivating words, Esperanza feels optimistic, and she also feels empowered in the world.

The neighborhood portrayed in *The House on Mango Street* shows the constant battle with Latino identity, the lack of support from the same culture and the burden and segregation involved in being a minority. Sandra Cisneros presents all the effects that the white-dominated world has on Latinos; it changes how other cultures think about Latino traditions and culture as a whole, and how Latinos in general think about themselves.

Conclusion

In Sheridan Blau's *The Literature Workshop: Teaching Texts and Their Readers,* he states that "one of the chief functions of a literature class is not to present literature to students (as conventional teaching guides are likely to advise) in ways that will anticipate and prevent their confusion, but to welcome and even foster among readers the experience of confusion" (Blau 2003). In working with underrepresented students, it is crucial that we do our best to guide them along a path with a gradual incline that leads to AP classes and instills in them the necessary skills for success at the university level. The strategies that I use to achieve this, discussed in this chapter, are as follows:

- Students need to be walked through *how* to discuss analysis and interpretation, including integrating textual references, blending analysis and interpretation, connective tissue, and linking their body paragraphs back to their thesis.
- Students need many opportunities to experiment with analysis and to discuss their interpretations in nonthreatening environments.
- Successful instruction in literary analysis requires us to place a much greater emphasis on prewriting than many underrepresented students currently receive.
- Students need frequent modeling of successful literary analysis.
- Students should gradually be moved along a continuum of scaffolding and support toward independently reading and analyzing cold texts.
- Students need explicit instruction in annotating text.
- Students should be given frequent opportunities to read and evaluate sample papers.

CHAPTER FOUR

Autobiographical and Biographical Writing Strategies: Using Students' Lives to Engage Them in Writing and School

MUCH OF THE RESEARCH ON STUDENTS OF COLOR INDICATES THAT THE SCHOOL SYSTEM TOO OFTEN DEVALUES THEIR EXPERIENCES, WHICH CAN BE QUITE DIFFERENT FROM THOSE OF MAINSTREAM STUDENTS. HOWEVER, AS ANY GOOD TEACHER KNOWS, WHEN A STUDENT WRITES ABOUT A SUBJECT THAT HE OR SHE PERCEIVES AS WORTHWHILE, THE ACT OF COMPOSING MOVES FROM A SOLELY ACADEMIC EXERCISE TO A MEANINGFUL PROCESS OF DISCOVERY AND EXPLORATION.

The genre of autobiographical writing can hold great appeal to underrepresented students because it values what too often is overlooked. As Sonia Nieto writes in her book *Affirming Diversity* (2007),

> Students' ability to develop literacy and other academic skills as traditionally defined by schools is necessary for academic success, but, if defined only in

this way, academic success is dysfunctional because it encourages students to abandon part of their identity in the process. Students' abilities to use the skills, talents, and experiences learned at home and in the community to further their learning must also be included in a definition of academic success.

Getting kids to write about themselves is not a problem, but getting them to write *well* about themselves is. After years of looking over student essays for college applications, I have noticed that writing about oneself presents a series of problems for many underrepresented students.

For one, too often students will choose the most traumatic event that has ever occurred in their lives as the focus of their paper. In my experience, many students have difficulty processing these events and do not really know what they wish to say about them, other than that they were painful.

The best autobiographical papers, however, have been those that take the more ordinary events in a person's life and examine them, offering some insight into everyday occurrences. Of course, it is very difficult to get students to reflect on their lives and draw insights from the events they experience. So, in this chapter I offer some strategies for getting students to write reflective pieces without becoming overwhelmed.

The Neighborhood Essay

As I have mentioned before, many underrepresented students feel as if their backgrounds and lives do not match up with those of the characters in the anthologies or novels used in the classroom. When we allow students to deal with the stuff of their lives in an academic setting, it fuels their interest in writing and eliminates many of the barriers to academic success. Therefore, I often try to get my students to talk and write about their world.

One way I accomplish this is through the first autobiographical foray, a short descriptive paper called the neighborhood essay. In a nutshell, I simply ask students to share their neighborhoods in a piece of writing—they may choose to discuss all of Anaheim, or just their household, or deal with something in between the two—and use this piece to focus on some of the elements of good autobiographical writing. Specifically, we focus on sensory detail and allowing a thesis to control the paper, a concept that will be important as we continue writing other college-preparatory pieces.

The first draft is incredibly rough. I simply ask students to tell me about their neighborhood. Johnny, my energetic, intelligent future leader, hands in this draft:

The reason why we are moving is because we are trapped in our own house. We can never go play in the front yard because we live on a busy street and my parents are afraid of us going in the street. We can't even go play in the back alley because people speed and race there. The only place we have is inside our house and our backyard. We are trapped in our house. That is the reason why we are moving.

One of the difficulties of working with students from a lower socioeconomic background is the too-frequent upheavals that occur in their home lives. No specific chapter in this book attempts to solve this problem because it is part of the student's situation and therefore part of my job. Saddened, I continue looking through the initial drafts of my students' papers, appreciating them for their honesty and frequent optimism.

The next day we work on descriptive writing. The students work through the following mini-lesson in their writer's notebooks. Simply put, students take vague, general statements and replace them with specific statements that carry descriptive detail.

Directions: Rewrite the sentences below, adding descriptive detail. The first one has been done for you as an example.

1. His stuff was lying all over the bed, the posters were sagging on the wall, and yesterday's lunch lay on the floor.
   His crumpled flannel shirts and torn jeans lay on the bed underneath the sagging posters of forgotten basketball stars; the flies swarming around yesterday's stale pizza seemed not to notice.
2. The car crashed into a wall.
3. We entered the dance and saw all of our friends.
4. The teacher seemed really mean and gave me an angry look.
5. She was beautiful (or) he was gorgeous.

Students then begin to brainstorm sensory details about their neighborhoods. At this stage, I introduce the concept of an implicit thesis and ask them to look at their ideas to see if there are any central elements that seem to stand out. If so, I encourage students to brainstorm further to come up with more details that support this central idea. Finally, students are asked to write a second draft, this time describing their neighborhoods with a specific central idea in mind rather than simply telling the reader random information about it. To assist with their writing, I share a couple of paragraphs from my own essay:

As I jog through the quiet street, the soft blue lights emanating from hundreds of television sets nestled in cookie-cutter houses wash the street, reminding me that I am indeed living in suburbia. My breathing grows heavy from running, and I can see the exhalations curl up in front of me, mingling with the late night fog that envelops the small, two-hill community every night.

Hordes of tightly packed houses in a wide range of beiges line my pathway. The cars in the various driveways—SUVs, four-door sedans, and mini-vans—proclaim that families occupy the houses, and those families are at home, inside. My family, like those of my neighbors, also sits bathed by the azure waters of TV right now.

After looking at my sample, students draft their own, and then I put a few up on the ELMO for us to respond to. Figure 4.1 is Destiny's draft, which we looked at as a class. As we read her paper, the students and I asked questions and made comments, which I've written next to each corresponding paragraph.

Figure 4.1 Destiny's Draft Neighborhood Essay

Destiny Ledesma	
Per. 3 11/29/06	
Where I live is not exactly Beverly Hills but it is not Compton neither, it is just a close nit community that I call home.	Can you add more to engage the reader here? Is your thesis that your neighborhood isn't real nice but it isn't real bad either?
The community in which I reside in is La Colonia Indepedencia. It is a community that consists of four streets, Berry, Garza, Harcourt, and Gilbert. The community is located between Gilbert and Pacific Place. The vast majority of its residents are Hispanic. On weekends, you could smell the aroma of BBQ's and the screaming of children and teenagers playing in the streets. Located at the corner of Berry Avenue and Pacific Place there is Esther E. Walter School this is the school in which all children form my community attend from kindergarten through sixth grade. I myself was too a former Walter school student. To the North of Pacific Place there are railroad tracks used by Southern Pacific Railroad. Everyday like clockwork at 8:00 a.m. you could hear the conductor bearing down on the whistle as it approaches Gilbert Street, and once more when it gets to Magnolia Street. Another site in my community would be the Magnolia School District Bus Service. Every morning at 7:00 a.m. I am awaken to the sound of buses leaving to pick up children for school. Though, every night before I go to sleep it is guaranteed that I will hear at least one siren or see one cop car go by. In closing, there is never a moment in my neighborhood where something is not going on.	Why do you tell us the streets that surround it? Is that information needed? Can you add more description that supports your thesis? Should the information about school be in a separate paragraph? Do you want the reader to see this as a good thing or a bad thing? Maybe make the bus information a separate paragraph. Your neighborhood seems safe but with some scary elements in it. Is that an effect you're trying to give the reader? This last line doesn't seem to go with the rest of this paragraph.
However, like all communities there are some troubles in paradise. For example, across the street from Gilbert there is a long brick wall that can most of the time can be seen with graffiti all over the wall and on the curbs as well. Also late at night there are teenagers as well as young adults hanging out on street corners. Occasionally, there are random gunshots, sometimes followed by sirens. Usually after 9:00 p.m. there are very few, if any people that hang out, outside there homes. To sum up, my community is not perfect, but even with these problems I still fell secure with the environment I am in.	Good details. This paragraph is all about the stuff that happens that's bad or dangerous. Is your thesis that La Colonia Indepedencia is scary on the surface but a safe family for those that live there?

Destiny Ledesma (cont.)	
In my community, we consider each other family; we all look out for one another. Most of us in my community are related to each other in way or another. Located on Garza is the heart of my community it is our community center. In the community center, they offer food to seniors as well as anyone who needs a helping hand. They give can food, cereals, bread, and cheese and around Christmas, they give out presents to all children that signed up. When there is a death in my community, all of my community comes to together to help the grieving family. After the burial there is a reception in which people donate a hot dish like chicken, tamales, rice, beans or anything to show a sign of love. In my community, there is a sense of unity and comfort. I am very well known in my community, in the summer time I sell Snow Cones in which all the little kids and adults come to buy. Overall, my community is just a well-rounded place to live no matter what blemishes it may have.	Show more of this security that you feel. So even though it's kind of dangerous, it's still a real family community ? Why do you mention this information? How does it support your thesis?
In closing, most would say my community is not the best place to live, but to it is the only place I feel secure, it is the only place I can call home.	If this is your thesis, then some of the body needs to be changed to match up with it.

After responding to Destiny's draft, the students work on revising their own, focusing on the thesis and on incorporating descriptive language. By the time Destiny finished her paper, she had done the following:

- Begun with a free write that allowed her to begin thinking about her neighborhood
- Practiced working with sensory details
- Drafted her essay
- Listened to questions and suggestions from her classmates
- Conferred with her instructor
- Revised, focusing on thesis and unity
- Solicited input from other students
- Revised according to feedback from other students
- Turned in a draft for me to comment on
- Revised according to my comments
- Published a final draft, which is included here

Destiny's final draft:

As I stroll to the front of my yard, pass the gigantic black gate that shadows eight feet above me, with a large key lock that offers some reassurance. The rusty bars signal it is a veteran of many years. A grating noise of unoiled hinges speaks to parents, informing them of any unwanted guest, also a warning to those who dare try to surpass its powerful iron bars. From the outside it looks like a solid black bard structure of a prison cell but from the inside a feeling of security.

The community in which I reside in is La Colonia Indepedencia. A rectangular shaped community consists of four streets, Berry, Garza, Harcourt, and Gilbert. The community is located between Gilbert and Pacific Place. The vast majority of its residents are Hispanic. When I walk outside my house on weekends to take out the trash, I can smell the aroma of BBQ and hear the sound of lawns being cut. When I walk to my grandma's house, I can see the screaming children and teenagers playing football in the streets. At the corner of Berry Avenue and Pacific Place, there is Esther E. Walter School. It is a small elementary school with a newly renovated playground that is filled with rubber chips that feel like the rubber of a tire. This is the school in which all the little children from my community attend from kindergarten through sixth grade. I myself was too a former Walter school student. To the North of Pacific Place there are old rusty railroad tracks that rattle when they are used by Southern Pacific Railroad. Everyday like clockwork at 8:00 a.m. you could hear the elderly conductor bearing down on the whistle that sounds like a fog horn as it approaches Gilbert Street, and once more when it gets to Magnolia Street. The conductor smiles and waves to the little children and their parents as they walk to school. In the middle of Berry Street across the street from my grandma's house is the Magnolia School District Bus Service. Before it was the Magnolia Bus Service, it used to be the school in which my grandfather attended. Every morning at 7:00 a.m. I am awaken to the sound of buses leaving to pick up children for school and baby birds chirping as they wait for their mothers to bring back breakfast. Every night as I lay down to go to sleep I am haunted by the sound of loud ghost like noises made by the fire trucks as they whisk by my house. In closing, there is never a moment in my neighborhood where something is not going on.

However, like all communities there are some troubles in paradise. For example, across the street form Gilbert there is a long, beige brick wall that can most of the time be seen with freshed painted graffiti all over the paint chipped wall and all over the chipped curbs

73

as well. In the afternoon, there are teenagers as well as young adults hanging out at street corners on their four- wheeled beach cruisers with their stereos in the back blasting oldies that can be heard a street away. Occasionally, in the middle of the night there are sounds of loud random gunshots, like firecrackers but these are much deadlier and sometimes followed by the haunting sounds of sirens. After 9:00 p.m., my community looks like the site of an abandoned ghost town. To sum up, my community is not perfect, but even with these problems I still fell secure with the environment I am in.

In my community, we consider each other family; we all look out for one another. Most of us in my community are related to each other in way or another. Located on Garza is the heart of my community it is our community center. In the community center, they offer food to seniors as well as anyone who needs a helping hand. They give can food, cereals, bread, and cheese and around Christmas, they give out presents to all children that signed up. When there is a death in my community, all of my community comes to together to help the grieving family. After the burial there is a reception in which people donate a hot dish like chicken, tamales, rice, beans or anything to show a sign of love. In my community, there is a sense of unity and comfort. I am very well known in my community, in the summer time I sell Snow Cones in which all the little kids and adults come to buy. Overall, my community is just a well-rounded place to live no matter what blemishes it may have.

The paper works for two basic reasons: it allows students to bring their worlds into the realm of academia, which too often overlooks the communities to which underrepresented students belong, and it allows students time to think through and reflect on something that they know firsthand. These aspects of the assignment cause Danielle to reflect, "I liked writing the neighborhood essay because I got to write about something that I love and know a lot about," and for Cuper to explain, "I got an opportunity to describe where I live and how I look at my neighborhood. I also liked for other people to see how I look at my neighborhood."

This idea that the papers were written so that others would read them was evident as we worked through the drafting process. Students were quick to have others read and respond to their compositions, much more so than usual. Another advantage of this paper is that students begin to analyze their own surroundings, an important step as they consider engaging in the world beyond their immediate neighborhood.

For example, Lucia writes that the neighborhood essay "made me realize how many more good things are in my neighborhood than bad ones. It got me thinking I really do live in a safe place compared to other places," while Rubia commented in her reflections that

> The neighborhood essay was a fun way to really notice what is around you. Sometimes people do not notice that there are many interesting things happening where they live. For instance, I had not noticed that my street was very kid friendly. Like when the Disneyland fireworks start at 9:30 at night, all the parents and their kids are out to watch them. I started to notice the smells in the morning and the sounds. I never took my time to realize those things.

Again, giving students the freedom to explore their own world as a stepping-stone to the world of academia and eliminating the intimidation factor in the earlier stages of the writing process produces better products in the long run.

Autobiographical Prewriting: The Lifemap

Two basic elements make autobiographical writing successful: the description of the event being discussed, and the insight that the description offers. A well-told story with no point frustrates most readers. Therefore, I try to frontload autobiographical writing with lots of opportunities to reflect on the thesis. The first activity I use is that of a lifemap, a metaphoric representation of a student's journey through life. I ask the students to list on a sheet of paper at least ten events in their life that they have learned from or that have affected them in some way. They then get to work drawing a lifemap that incorporates all ten of these events plus any others that they would like to include. One example is shown in Figure 4.2.

Figure 4.2 Sample Lifemap

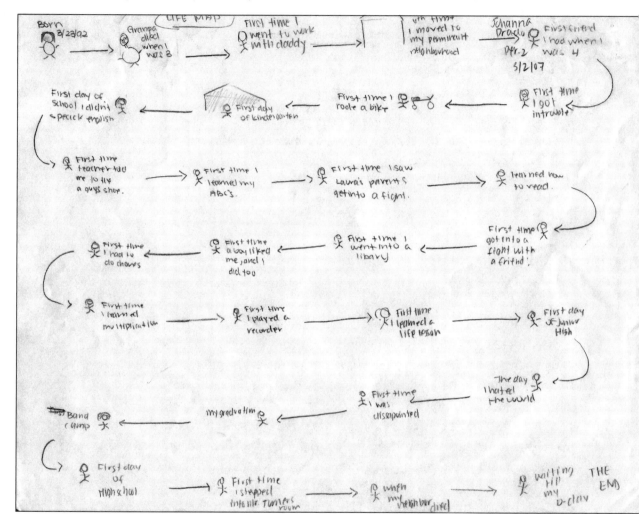

When they are finished, I have students write their insights: How did each event affect them? What did they learn from each event? What should others understand about life after having heard about this event?

The important aspect of this activity is that students at some point reflect on what they have learned from each event. Many of the items that they choose for their lifemaps are too laden with emotions or are too traumatic for them to process intellectually. Students are encouraged to use some of the events in their lifemap for their writer's notebook essays in order to figure out which ones would make good papers.

The Backward Map

Similar to the lifemap, the backward map assignment asks students to reflect on events from their lives. However, for this activity we start at the end: what are some lessons that you have learned in life, or what are some beliefs that you hold? On the right side of their paper, students list lessons/beliefs that they have acquired throughout their lives. After generating several qualities/ beliefs, they then choose a few of the items on their list and identify either when or where they learned each lesson or acquired each belief, or they iden- tify an event from their lives that illustrates the lesson or belief. The goal here is to get students to reflect on their lives. See Figure 4.3 for an example of a backward map.

Figure 4.3 Sample Backward Map

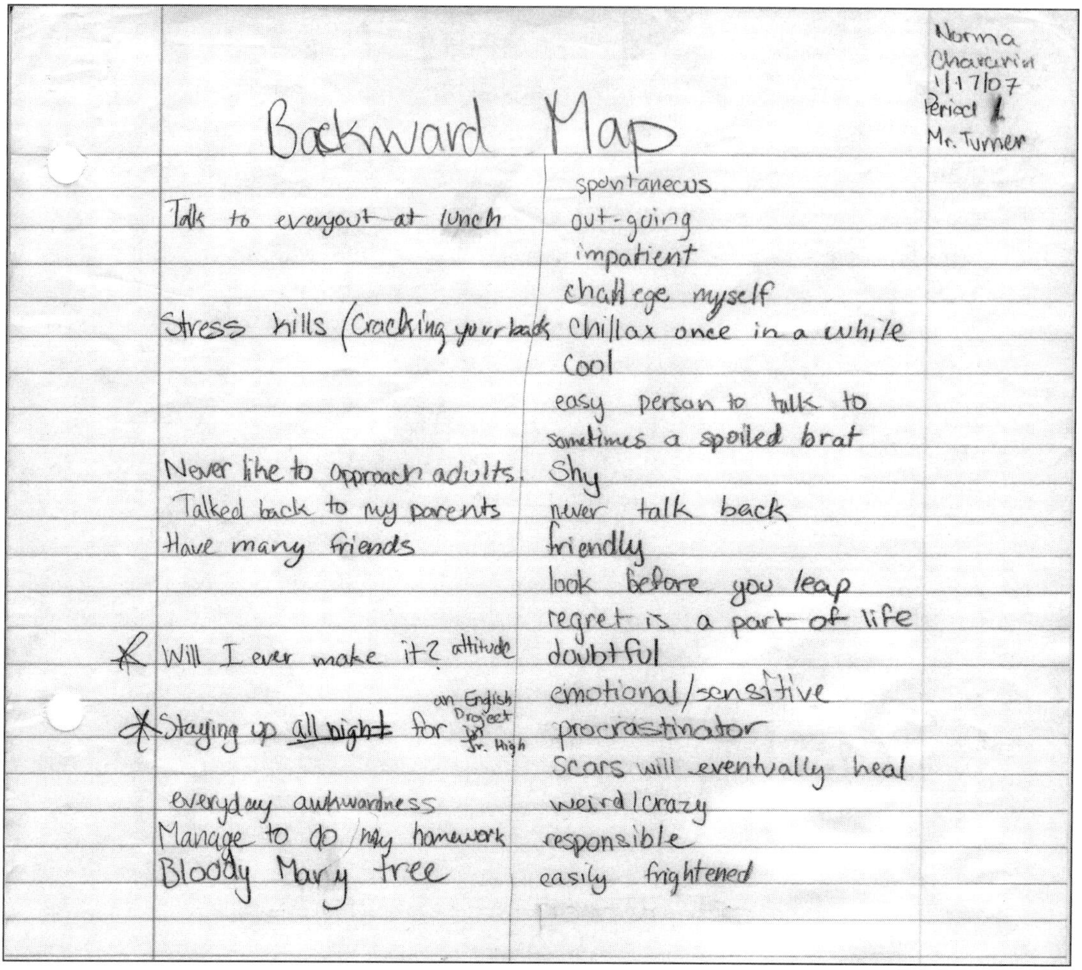
Norma Chavarin
1/17/07
Period 1
Mr. Turner

Backward Map

	spontaneous
Talk to everyout at lunch	out-going
	impatient
	challege myself
Stress kills (Cracking your back	Chillax once in a while
	Cool
	easy person to talk to
	sometimes a spoiled brat
Never like to approach adults.	Shy
Talked back to my parents	never talk back
Have many friends	friendly
	look before you leap
	regret is a part of life
* Will I ever make it? attitude	doubtful
	emotional/sensitive
* Staying up all night for an English Project Jr. High	procrastinator
	Scars will eventually heal
everyday awkwardness	weird/crazy
Manage to do my homework	responsible
Bloody Mary free	easily frightened

The Autobiography Prewrite

Once my writers have chosen their thesis, and the story that they are going to tell to convey that thesis, they fill out a graphic organizer to help organize their paper. They write down their thesis on the bottom of the page and the event itself on the top of the page, followed by a list of the main elements of the incident—important characters, locations, etc. Underneath each of the main elements of their story, I have them do quick brainstorms of the needed sensory details.

Too frequently, students will just begin drafting their events without a plan, which results in distracting and unnecessary information, a meandering narrative structure, and a lack of specific detail. Forcing students to focus on their thesis throughout the writing process and requiring them to plan each aspect of the paper helps them to produce an autobiographical piece that is rich in detail and meaning.

Figure 4.4 shows Norma's autobiography prewrite.

Figure 4.4 Sample Autobiography Prewrite

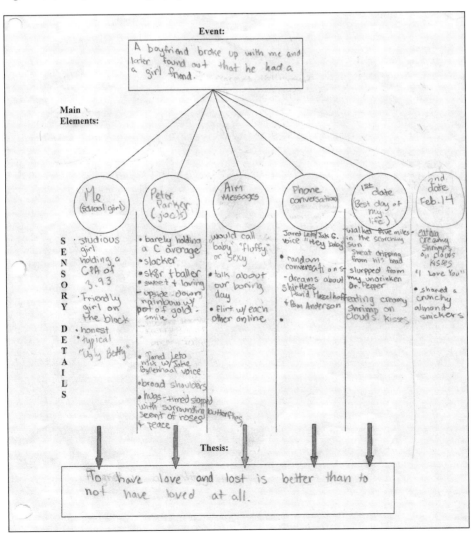

Thesis Mini-lesson

From the lifemap, backward map, and the first-draft essays from their writer's notebooks, students are asked to select a specific event that affected them. At this stage, students are asked to brainstorm sensory details that are associated with the event, keeping in mind their thesis.

Before we begin drafting, it is necessary to get students to focus on the importance of having a thesis. In groups, students are asked to read the following two passages, both of which are very poorly written. One, however, has a thesis; the other one does not. Students are asked to determine which one has a central idea and which one is still in search of a point.

SCOPE PARAGRAPHS

1. My best friend's name is Angela. She is 5'4" and has long brown hair. We met while at school, and I've learned a great deal through our friendship.

While at a club, a guy named Julio came over to us and started talking to both of us. I thought he was cute and wanted to ask him for his number, but he seemed more interested in her. Strangely enough, though, Angela answered him with curt responses and made it very difficult for him to talk to her. I couldn't figure out what was going on. After a few minutes, Julio walked away, puzzled by Angela's strange behavior.

After he left, I asked Angela why she had acted that way toward him. She replied that she could tell that I liked him and would rather not take the risk of damaging our friendship. A tidal wave of gratitude washed over me, then, and I realized what a truly special friend Angela was to sacrifice a chance with a guy in order to protect a friendship with me.

I've never forgotten that moment. Even today, when I'm faced with choices like whether or not to go out with my boyfriend or go out with Angela, I'll try and make sure that either I see Angela or make other arrangements so that she knows I still value her friendship. This attitude of protecting the friendships I already have has become very important to me, and as a result, I think it has made me a better friend to others, as well.

2. My best friend's name is Angela. She is 5'4" and has long brown hair. We met while at school, and we've always had a great friendship. We've never been in a fight.

While at a club, a guy named Julio came over to us and started talking to both of us. I thought he was cute and wanted to ask him for his number, but he seemed more interested in her. Strangely enough, though, Angela answered him with curt responses and made it very difficult for him to talk to her. I couldn't figure out what was going on. After a few minutes, Julio walked away, puzzled by Angela's strange behavior.

After he left, I asked Angela why she had acted that way toward him. She replied that she could tell that I liked him and would rather not take the risk of damaging our friendship. I couldn't believe she had done that for me and I was very glad she had, even though I never saw Julio again.

Angela has been my best friend ever since. We've experienced good times and bad times, but we've never turned against each other or been mean to each other. I don't know whatever happened to Julio. Angela has been a good friend to me and always will be in my heart.

Students discuss the two passages and share their views. Most groups correctly identify the first passage as the one with a thesis.

Samples for Discussion

Prior to writing the autobiographical paper, students are asked to read two sample papers. As we read the papers, students discuss in small groups the strengths of each paper and how it can be improved. The following is a transcript from this year's conversation (*S* stands for *student*):

TURNER: What did you think of the first paper?

S1: I liked it.

TURNER: Why?

S1: The descriptions were really good. You could picture it in your mind and it sounded collegiate.

TURNER: Where do you see good descriptions?

S2: The part about the water lilies trapped in her eyelashes . . .

S3: The gunshots of the drunk guys at the bar.

S4: The photograph was really described good, too.

TURNER: OK, so she described her images well. Any other sensory details besides visual?

S2: The smell of the ranch, the sound of the gunshots.

S3: The cold water, that's feeling.

S5: The photograph . . . oh wait, never mind.

TURNER: What else did you like about the paper?

S6: She had good sentences.

TURNER: What do you mean by that?

S6: She sounded smart the way she wrote her sentences.

S3: She used a lot of the different sentence styles in her paper.

S1: I kind of didn't get the ending though.

S3: I thought she was saying that death is kind of bad but in a way good because you learn from it about life . . . like you appreciate people and see them differently because of the pain of someone else dying . . . Yeah, something like that.

TURNER: So in terms of scope, did you feel as if the writer had something insightful to share?

S3: Definitely.

TURNER: What about the other paper, the one about the ambulance?

S1: That one sucked.

S7: It was like, one essay at the beginning and then another subject at the end and neither one really mattered. Like it didn't have a point to it . . .

S4: There was no thesis.

S1: Did a Puente student write this?

S8: What grade did it get?

TURNER: Wait, in what exact areas do you think it needed improvement?

S8: Everything.

S3: No thesis.

S2: There's no descriptions anywhere. You don't feel like you're there.

S1: It's boring.

TURNER: So what advice would you give this writer?

S8: Go back into rehab.

S2: Get better descriptions . . . Use the senses.

S4: Try to include something they learned from the event.

S7: The beginning is really bad, too. I would try to start by describing the accident and then tell the rest of the story.

These open conversations in class, where students discuss the merits and weaknesses of writing in a safe environment, add much to the students' perceptions of what makes good writing.

Narrative Introductions

Students unused to narrative writing will often want to use introductions styled after the expository writing more frequently done in history classes. Often, they will place their thesis in the introduction when it is not always needed there in this genre. Students need to see multiple examples of different ways to begin their autobiographical pieces. What I have done for the past several years is to have them focus on the story aspect of their autobiographical piece, then go back and work the introduction at the end.

What follow are some examples that I present to the students as they begin to work on their introductions with the goal of engaging the reader from the very first sentence. After continuing to draft their introductions for homework, the following day we all read our narrative introductions to the rest of the class, so that each student hears the strategies used by others in the class.

TYPES OF NARRATIVE INTRODUCTIONS

The Dramatic Lead

Every once in a while, when we got together for Sunday dinner, my older brother would glare at me from across the table. My heart would sink, for I knew full well what that look meant.

Starting in the Middle of a Scene

The oncoming driver swerved to avoid the deer and ended up in my lane, headlights blaring in my eyes. I looked at my girlfriend, hoped that I would live to see her again, and that was the last memory I have of that fateful day.

Starting with Dialogue

"Where's Dad going with my dog?" I cried.

The Funnel Lead

The week before Christmas signals a change throughout the sociological landscape of Los Angeles. Skyscrapers offer neon celebratory dances while traffic builds on the sidestreets, bathing the city in a sea of red brake lights. Individuals move to and fro, dressed in stylish jeans and light tee-shirts. At 1211 Lankersheim Avenue, the Los Angeles Christmas seems far removed, foreign even, from the childhood memories of Kelly Spaulding.

Beginning at the Ending

As they laid my mother's casket into the ground, I thought back to how carefree and wild our lives were just one year earlier.

The Mysterious Lead

She was black like soy sauce, her eyes the green of peeled seedless grapes.

Introduce the Narrator

At first glance, I don't seem any different than any other happy, suburban homeowner.

Beginning with the Setting

Cobwebs. Darkness. Cold stones. The squeaking of rats. The smell of dung. My terror had just begun.

Revising the Autobiographical Paper

After students have put together a draft, conferred with their peers and me, and then made changes according to those responses, they turn in their papers. I will read each paper and respond as if I were grading the paper for a final time. When students get the papers back, they receive comments without a grade. They then have a week to revise their papers according to my feedback; we will usually devote one or two days to a writer's workshop-type format during which students can confer further with each other or with me.

Figure 4.5 shows Johanna's paper, with comments from me and from her fellow writers.

Figure 4.5 Sample Draft Autobiographical Paper

Johanna Prado
Puente English
Period: 2
2/23/07

Autobiographical

good intro

Crying, laughing, and running. This is the last I remember of Rosa. I turned and looked at my friends, and they were laughing as Rosa was running away. Right then and there I felt I was on top of the world because of what power I had over her. I couldn't believe how upset she came to be; she must have thought that running away might solve her problems.

revise

One month earlier, it was the day I ~~scant~~ *can't* easily forget. A new girl from out of nowhere ~~just~~ came into the class, and she ~~just~~ stood ~~there~~ *quietly* next to Mrs. Kelly's desk. Then I noticed that she was wearing black converse, just the ones I wanted. She was wearing new *(w)pants* clothes, although she didn't seem to care, and that infuriated me. Her hair was pulled

see me

back in a perfect bun~~; although I didn't take notice in things such as hair,~~ I ~~decided to take notices and envy her.~~ To make matters worse, she had beautiful almond shaped eyes, and her eye color was caramel with some green. Just as the perfect lighting hit her lips, they seemed to sparkle just as the water does. While she was walking to her new seat, it seemed like her lips glistened as she spoke to the teacher. *and i begin to envy her.* ~~Other than her appearance she had taken a seat~~ *Sitting* next to me, ~~and~~ *she* seemed ~~the least bit~~ *an* excited. The usual routine went on, and when it was time to answer questions, she had answered them all correctly. I

italicize see me

remember thinking to myself, "Who does she think she is, I am the smart one in this class, and I am not about to let this so-called girl get in my way." I let her off easy since it was her first day at Disney Elementary. The teacher as usual always announced new people before recess. It happed that her name was Rosa, but I was too busy not caring to ever hear her name. I was asked by the teacher to stay in class so she could talk to me, and I did. As soon as the teacher was done talking to me, I ran outside to enjoy the rest of my recess, but as soon as I stepped foot outside the door I saw something despicable. The new girl was talking to my friends, and my friends seemed to enjoy talking to her. I was not going to take this any longer, so I marched up to her and ~~patted~~ poked her on the back. Immediately she turned around and I said, "I know you are the new girl, so I am going to be easy on you today. Now leave my sight." As indicating the end of The bell rang meaning that recess was over, although still How can I make these sentences flow better I was no longer upset, ~~in an essence~~ I pretty much despised her. Finally the bell rang once more, releasing us from school.

Recess came by so quickly and again the teacher wised to speak to me before I had a chance to go outside. Once more I went outside to once again see the same incidence happen. I finally couldn't take it many more and decided to march up to the new girl, and instead of patting her on the back, I completely turned her around. She was forced to look at me straight into the eyes. I bellowed, "What do you think you are doing talking to my friends, wait don't answer. Didn't I clearly tell you yesterday to stay away from my friends!? Why don't you go back to San Francisco! No one likes you here. You think that you are all that, but sweetie you need a reality check and you are not all that. Now go on and leave me and my friends alone, you are such a loner." My friends giggled as I saw tears run down Rosa's face. At that moment, I felt like I had put her in her place; she deserved what I had just done. I took notice that Rosa just stood there paralyzed, but I didn't stop there, I said, "Run along loser!" she immediately ran off into the class room. my friends and I The bell rang as me and my friends headed off to class to soon face the consequences, our anticipated ~~but it was so worth the punishment~~. To my surprise the teacher went on with her lessons, and Rosa was nowhere in sight. It was as if the ground had sucked her in. It was obvious

the new girl had left school early. ~~It was time again to go home~~.

It was finally Wednesday, ~~just happens to be my favorite weekday~~, and the new girl

was still nowhere in sight. I remember commenting to my friends, "She must still be

crying form yesterday, what a loser." The day went on as usual, and it was time to leave

school. My mom ~~as usual~~ asked me how school went, and I ~~always~~ answered nothing. *see me*

① Then I told my mom that I had not seen the new girl at school today. My mom knew that

the new girl was just sick, but she told me that ~~"~~ the new girl ~~had~~ has moved back to San

Francisco. ~~She said that I shouldn't~~ and don't call her the new girl, because she had a name. I didn't

bother to listen to what my mom had to say about her. Mom said ~~that I had my~~ "you have a worried

face on," and I just ignored her comment. Then she said ~~that I~~ "you looked nervous, or even

scared." ② She must have thought that I had done something to the new girl to have made her

leave, so I said "I didn't do anything to make her leave." She rolled her eyes at me, so I ran

to my bedroom. By dinner time I had decided to confess my sin to my mother. In a

squeaky voice I said, " I may have said some mean things to make her mad, but not

anything to make her want to go back home." She made her ~~face~~ Facial expression that

screamed out; yeah right you know what you said. Her face expression soon after

changed to a disappointed face, and I decided to skip dinner that night. I soon after drifted

into a deep slumber, and for a moment I envisioned Rosa smiling at me, but that picture

soon changed into her crying a river. Just like that I had wakened up to my room, and it

was another day for school.

I arrived at school, and everybody was talking about the new girl, and I was just

ignoring everything. I had been feeling sick to my stomach, and I thought that it would

88

soon vanish, but my stomachache didn't vanish. I was felling like a jerk, and I just

decided to take a seat on the swings. I really felt terrible for not being able to apologize. I

was to the point where I was going to cry. Then I felt somebody tap me on the shoulder,

up to see

and I looked and it was Rosa. I quickly stated, "What are you doing here, I thought you

see me

moved back to San Francisco." She then said, "No, I was just sick, but I was thinking

abut moving back home just like you had said." I said I was sorry and she said that she

understood, and that it was cool between us. My friends ran over to us, and they started

— show

saying things to make Rosa feel insignificant, and this time I stood up for her. My friends

were shocked at me, and they said that I was not their friend anymore, but I didn't care I

— dash

was not in the mood. I learned a very important lesson that day; never trust your parents,

ha-
see me

just kidding, don't make the same mistake twice. You might not have a second chance to

say you're sorry.

it seems as if your thesis should be different — see me

rework conclusion

Days went by and I had gotten along with Rosa, but he story ends here. Remember to

never make the same mistake twice. You might not have a second chance to correct your

mistakes, and you could miss out in a lot.

Final Draft—Johanna

The following is the final draft that Johanna turned in. As with all papers done in the Puente class, students are allowed to rewrite for a higher score if they would like.

JOHANNA PRADO

PUENTE ENGLISH

PERIOD: 2

AUTOBIOGRAPHICAL

Crying, laughing, and running, this is the last I remember of Rosa. As I turned around, I looked at my friends, and they were laughing as Rosa was running away. Right then and there I felt I was on top of the world because of what power I had over her. I couldn't believe how upset she came to be; she must have thought that running away might solve her problems, or at least save herself from that moment.

One month earlier, it was the day I can never forget, the day *she* arrived. A new girl from out of nowhere just came into the class, and she quietly stood next to Mrs. Kelly's desk. Then I noticed that she was wearing black converse, exactly the ones I wanted. She was also wearing new Levi pants, she didn't seem to care, and that infuriated me. Her hair was pulled back in a perfect bun. To make matters worse, she had beautiful almond shaped eyes, her eye color was caramel brown with light green. Just as the perfect lighting hit her lips, they seemed to sparkle just as the water did. While she was walking to her new seat, it seemed like her lips glistened as she spoke to the teacher, and I began to envy her. Sitting next to me, she seemed unexcited. The usual routine went on, and when it was time to answer questions she had answered them all correctly. I remember thinking to myself, *who does she think she is? I am the smart one in this class, and I am not about to let this so called girl get in my way!* I let her off easy since it was her first day at Disney Elementary. The teacher as usual always announced new people before recess. It happed that her name was Rosa, but I was too busy not caring to ever hear her name. I was asked by the teacher to stay in class so she could talk to me, and I did. As soon as the teacher was done talking to me, I ran outside to enjoy the rest of my recess, but as soon as I stepped foot outside the door I saw something despicable. The new girl was talking to *my* friends, and *my* friends seemed to enjoy talking to *her*. I was not going to take this any longer, so I marched up to her and lightly tapped her on the back.

Immediately she turned around and announced to her, "I know you are the new girl, so I am going to be easy on you today. Now leave my sight." The bell rang indicating the end of recess, I was no longer upset, although I pretty much despised her. Thankfully the new girl had to leave school early, and lunch was more peaceful. Finally the bell rang once more, releasing us from school.

Recess came by so quickly, and again the teacher wanted to speak to me, before I had a chance to go outside. Once more I went outside to again see the same incidence happen. I finally couldn't take it many more and decided to march up to the new girl, and instead of patting her on the back, I completely turned her around. She was forced to look at me straight into the eyes.

I bellowed, "What do you think you are doing talking to my friends, wait don't answer. Didn't I clearly tell you yesterday to stay away from my friends!? Why don't you go back to San Francisco! No one likes you here. You think that you are all that, but sweetie you need a reality check, you are *not* all that! Now go on and leave me and *my* friends alone, you loner!" My friends giggled as we saw tears run down Rosa's face. At that moment, I felt like I had put her in her place; she deserved what I had just done. I took notice that Rosa just stood there paralyzed, but I didn't stop there I said, "Run along loser!" she immediately ran off into the class room. The bell rang, my friends and I headed off to class to soon face our anticipated consequences. To my surprise, the teacher went on with her lessons, and Rosa was nowhere in sight. It was as if the ground had sucked her in. It was obvious the new girl had left school early.

It was finally Wednesday, and the new girl was still nowhere in sight. I remember commenting to my friends, "She must still be crying from yesterday, what a loser." The day went on as usual and it was time to leave school. My mom had asked me how school went, but I shrugged in silence.

Then I told my mom that I had not seen the new girl at school today. My mom knew that the new girl was just sick, but she said, "The new girl moved back to San Francisco, and don't call her the new girl, because she has a name. I didn't bother to listen to what my mom had to say about her. Mom said, "You have your worried face on," and I just ignored her comment. Then she said, "You look nervous, or even scared."

She must have thought that I had done something to the new girl to have made her leave, so I said, "I didn't do anything to make her leave." She rolled her eyes at me, so I ran to my bedroom.

By dinner time I had decided to confess my sin to my mother. In a squeaky voice I said, "I may have said some mean things to make her mad, but not anything to make her want to go back home." She made her facial expression that screamed out; yeah right you know what you said. Her facial expression soon after changed to a disappointed face, and I decided to skip dinner that night. I soon after drifted into a deep slumber, and for a moment, I envisioned Rosa smiling at me, but that picture soon changed into her crying a river. Just like that, I had wakened up to my room, and it was another day for school.

I arrived at school, and everybody was talking about the new girl, and I was just ignoring everything. I had been feeling sick to my stomach, and I thought that it would soon vanish, but my stomachache didn't vanish. I was feeling like a jerk, and I just decided to take a seat on the swings. I really felt terrible for not being able to apologize. I was to the point where I was going to cry. Then I felt somebody tap me on the shoulder, and I looked up to see Rosa.

I quickly stuttered, "W-what are you doing here, I thought you moved back to San Francisco!?"

She then stated, "No, I was just sick, but I was thinking abut moving back home just like you had said." I claimed I was sorry and she said that she understood, and that it was cool between us.

My friends ran over to us, and they started saying things to make Rosa feel insignificant, like I had once done, but I said, "Get a life, you don't need to pick on her in order to make yourselves feel better, besides Rosa has feelings too you know!"

They said, "You're funny, you're the one who was mean to her in the first place."

I declared, "I don't care! Now leave me and Rosa to alone, go on and ruin someone else's life." My friends were shocked at me, and they said that I was not their friend anymore, but I didn't care—I was definitely *not* in the mood. I learned a very important lesson that day; never trust your parents, just kidding, One should know who their friends truly are. Just because my friends were being mean to Rosa doesn't mean I have to follow there ways.

Days went by and I had gotten along with Rosa, but the story ends here. Remember I should know what kind of friends I have, because I might have not had a second chance to correct my mistakes. I could have missed out in having such a loyal friend, one like Rosa.

Introducing the Biographical Paper

After students have had some experience with autobiographical writing, we then tackle biographical writing. All Puente students at Magnolia High School read *Rain of Gold* by Victor Villaseñor during the summer between their freshman and sophomore years, which serves as an example of biographical writing for the students. *Rain of Gold* is an incredible novel that many consider to be the cornerstone of Chicano literature; most students love to read about the journey of Villaseñor's parents from Mexico to the United States. Some students begin to question their own family's experience and history as they read the novel. In fact, during the summer, students are asked to write a first draft of a biographical piece, which we later revise once school begins. The following is the biographical writing assignment, created by a team of Puente teachers during one of our yearly training conferences:

BIOGRAPHICAL NARRATIVE

Part One. The Interview.

After having read *Rain of Gold* (or perhaps while you read), consider your own family's story. Interview an older relative (parent, grandparent, uncle/aunt) about the journey that your family undertook to live in California. You may, of course, interview more than one relative in order to get as many details regarding the journey as possible. Here are some questions you might ask:

- Why did the people involved move to the United States?
- When did the move to the United States happen?
- How did the move to the United States happen?
- What obstacles were there throughout the journey?
- Who was/were the key figures in your family's history?
- What were some specific events that happened on the journey?
- Describe these events: what were some specific sights, sounds, smells, tastes, and/or physical feelings that your interviewee can remember about these events?
- How did the journey change the people involved?
- What qualities or skills enabled the people involved to succeed?

- How did life turn out for the people involved?
- What did the people involved learn from the journey?

Naturally, you'll want to ask lots of follow-up questions as well, such as "Why?" or "Tell me more about that." If you're talking to the actual person who made the journey, consider asking, "How do you feel about that now?" or "How do you feel about the decision to make the journey?"

Part Two. The Rough Draft.

After conducting your interview, write a biographical narrative of your family's journey. Make sure to use sensory detail, descriptive language, literary techniques, and most important, to focus on a theme/thesis. This is just like writing an auto-biographical paper, except that you're writing about someone else's life.

Your biographical paper should be typed or written on a computer. We will work on revising and editing your paper once we get back from summer.

Writing this kind of paper is powerful for underrepresented students. For many of my writers, this is the first time that they learn of their family's history as it relates to making the journey to America. The act of writing their family's story places many of them in an exalted position as they chronicle the events in a way that few others could or would. The honor that the paper does to the elder family members often brings my writers' great personal satisfaction and reward. I love my students' responses to this paper: the realization of the importance of their heritage. It is the first time many of my underrepresented students actually internalize the heroism of their family members. This inner growth that students experience after writing their parents' history moves many of my writers, like Angelica, who, after completing her biographical piece, wrote the following reflective response:

At first, when I knew that my Puente class had to write an essay about our family history, I thought "great, I have to write an essay over summer vacation." However, I'm glad that I wrote the essay because my eyes opened to hardships that I never knew my mom had endured, especially at such a young age. My mom's family economic hardship had driven her to risk her own life just to give a better life to her family. My mom's difficult experience has demonstrated to me that I should be grateful to live in the United States and should not allow any obstacle from restraining me to pursue an education. With her sacrifices, I am motivated to push myself to go beyond what my family expects from me; therefore, her hardships will allow me to have a successful life. Now, whenever I ask my mom about her family history, she ceases from her responsibilities and begins telling her story, while I listen with fascination.

Sample Biographical Paper

Students come back from their summer break with a rough draft of their biographical papers, which we then take through the writing process, reviewing narrative introductions and unity. After much sharing and responding, and conferencing with me, the final drafts are compiled into a class anthology of our journeys.

JEARELLY PINEDO

THE MOVE TO AMERICA

My mom; the woman I wake up to every day. The woman who raised me, loved me, and provided me with everything I've ever needed. Though, as she speaks to me of her past, the mom I once saw as just a shoulder to cry on, someone to love and a money generator becomes a powerful, forceful, memorable woman. Her gentle cotton-like lips unveil a story, one that captivates me. Her grip on the tablemat tightens; our eye contact diminishes as her eyes shift toward the floor. As we sit there at our rusty old table, I meet with the multi-color cheap plastic fruit centerpiece. Though as she continues, I begin to treasure the table, the centerpiece, and every other decoration on the walls I once referred to as tacky and worthless. As my appreciation for even these small items expands, her mouth lets out detail after detail of her journey to a new life.

The year was 1967 and America was the desired destination for many Latinos living in Mexico. Although Mexico was a decent place to live, America seemed to have roads paved of gold and the capability of opening more doors. Everyone saw it as the land of opportunities where everyone was treated fairly.

"Mama, are we ready?" asked Maria, patiently standing there in her pink-laced dress. Though she was only fourteen, she held the responsibilities of a mother.

"I believe so, mija. Grab Netito and tell the rest to start up the hill." Maria picked up her little brother and held him closely. She thought of the days where she was once this

95

innocent age—where there were no worries in the world, just following mom. Yet there was no time to reminisce for today was the memorable moment she'd hoped for since her early years, before she'd been piled up with the responsibility of her seven siblings. Her small shabby shack would be abandoned; she was going to America.

Today the cloudy and humid weather did not bother Maria the least bit, unlike other days where she preferred the sun and loathed the dark gray clouds. Her attitude evolved into something beautiful, where optimism was at its biggest existence. The image of her stout dark father and his honey-tinted eyes steadily paced back and forth in her head while he awaited the presence of his wife and eight children in the small rural town of Watsonville.

They were on their way, walking through the dusty rocky roads of Zacatecas. Maria occasionally caught herself walking at a greater speed than the others. She couldn't help it; she was overly excited about the move. Her dark chicken legs expressed this excitement in their brisk movement. She figured that if she picked up the pace, the others would as well. With everyone hustling, they would arrive at the bus station sooner, and in turn would have more time to settle in their new home, purchased by their father Roberto from a local farmer. Though as she'd turn back to glance at her mother struggling with Netitio in arms and the rest of the children, their flushed faces and heavy breathing caused Maria to slow down even if it meant arriving to the U.S. a little later than she had hoped for.

Preparation was of their least concern for even if they weren't able to bring along all their belongings, life was going to be all the brighter in the U.S. Not only would they be reunited with their father, but they also felt life overall would be simpler and divine at the same time.

The doors slid open and one by one Maria's family hopped on. This bus would take them to their desired location: America. Days passed and Maria and her family patiently waited with other America-bound families on the stuffy bus. Their diet consisted of mainly stale bread and warm water, which they had brought themselves, and the only time to relieve themselves was during short pit stops. Maria was grateful for all this because she was aware that this was all temporary and that things would soon progress; however, surprisingly frustration began to take over Maria. Her hopes and dreams were beginning to fade. Pessimism began to win her over. She began to think, *yes, my daddy promised us a home and a settled life, but how can I be so sure that he was telling the truth? What if he isn't even alive?* Her negativity increased more and more with the heat, the bumpy road, and the crowded atmosphere. Suddenly the bus came to a halt and at this moment Maria didn't know what to think. She met eyes with her mom who was exhausted yet managed to carry a smile.

So there they stood, Maria, her mom, and her large family. Unsure of their location, Maria looked around. No sign of her father. She wasn't sure of what was to happen, and her mother wasn't making matters any easier for she remained in complete silence. It seemed as if Maria was the mother and all the children were eyeing her so as to ask "What now?" Maria began to panic as she realized that at this point they had no shelter, they had no life. They might as well have stayed in Mexico because it seemed as if America had nothing to offer them. Her mother began to walk toward a narrow field without speaking a word. The silence tormented Maria's inquisitive mind; yet her mom continued walking so everyone followed. Maria spotted a tall white man approaching them. He greeted them in Spanish with a strong accent. After a difficult discussion, the family began to pick strawberries. Although she and the other children were not very fond of what was going on, she realized how lucky they were to just happen to bump into the head of the field that provided them with jobs, which meant that they had hope. That night her family went to sleep cold, hungry, and confused, with their dad and their expected home in mind.

The next morning, Maria awoke to the sound of soft mumbling. As her eyelids opened, she made out the figure of a short man standing there speaking with her mom. She got up and walked toward them; she saw that it was no other than her dad. He took a quick glance at her and immediately embraced her in his arms. The moment was unlike any other she had experienced. With all the commotion going on, the rest of the children awoke as well and hugged their father, except for the two younger ones who knew him as a stranger. Her dad led them to his small car. She was overwhelmed with pride. After the hour drive, they arrived in the small rural town of Watsonville. Maria looked around and there to the right was the warmest, most welcoming home she'd ever seen. "Well this is it," said her dad. They all got out and entered the house. She looked around, and although it wasn't as fancy as she'd expected, she felt special and she knew that the entire week of suffering had paid off. She would live in this house until she was eighteen. After five years of farming the fertile Northern soil of California, Maria married and accompanied her husband to the southern city of Anaheim.

This is the story of my mother. Her past makes me realize how easy I have it and how much I take for granted. My mother never had much; however, she always seemed to make the best of every small thing, even at the worst times. So as I sit here pondering her past, I am overtaken with a sense of optimism. I thank my mother for what she has accomplished—if it weren't for all her sacrifices, I would not be privileged with the opportunities I now have. She lived through hard times to make my life better and I thank her for that.

Conclusion

Writing about one's own experiences is so empowering that it can transform writers. To ask students to write about what they are familiar with, and to enable them to think critically about the events of their own lives and reflect on the value of their life experiences can engage reluctant writers and inspire them to write with passion. Giving underrepresented students the opportunity to delve into their own worlds and lives, which are too often not explored in academia, can make all the difference in a student's attitude toward writing, propelling the writer from apathy to motivation and from resistance to enthusiasm.

CHAPTER FIVE

Teaching Argument and Research Writing Strategies:

Here's a quick quiz to get us started:

1. In which of the following years was the abortion rate at its lowest? (Ventura et al. 2002)
   a) 1990, b) 1994, c) 1998, d) 2002, e) 2006

2. True or False: Latino pregnancy rates have decreased in recent years. (Ventura et al. 2002)

3. True or False: The rate of unintended births—unintended pregnancies carried to term—rose by 44 percent among poor women from 1994 to 2001, but declined by 8 percent for wealthier women. (Zernike 2006)

4. The percentage of Latinos who have attained their bachelor's degrees is (U.S. Census Bureau 2003):
   a) 3 percent, b) 7 percent, c) 10 percent, d) 33 percent, e) 50 percent

5. True or False: The percentage of Latinos who are living in poverty is higher today than it was ten years ago. (U.S. Census Bureau 2006)

6. True or False: Since 1994, violent crime rates have increased, reaching the highest level ever recorded in 2005. (U.S. Bureau of Justice Statistics, "Crime and Victims Statistics")

7. The number of children and youth homicides that are school-related make up what percent of the total number of homicides in the United States? (Department of Health and Human Services)
   a) 1 percent, b) 10 percent, c) 20 percent, d) 33 percent, e) 50 percent

99

8. From 1994 to 2006, illicit drug use (other than marijuana) among twelfth-graders has: (U.S. Bureau of Justice Statistics, "Crime and Victims Statistics")
   a) increased, b) stayed the same, c) decreased

9. In 2006, approximately what percentage of students in the United States took at least one Advanced Placement exam? (Farrell 2006)
   a) 8 percent, b) 16 percent, c) 23 percent, d) 33 percent, e) 50 percent

10. At NYU, when comparing the average SAT score for incoming freshmen of 1995 with 2000: (Weiss 2000)
    a) There was an increase of 52 points, b) there was a decrease of 52 points, c) the scores stayed about the same

11. In terms of IQ, today's students, when compared with their grandparents:
    a) score about the same, b) score about 18 points lower, c) score about 14 points higher (Berliner 1993)

ANSWERS:

1. The abortion rate has been steadily dropping every year since the early 1990s (answer e).

2. True. Latino pregnancy rates have decreased in the last ten years.

3. True. The rate of unintended pregnancy for poor women has increased while decreasing for wealthy women.

4. The percentage of Latinos who have attained their bachelor's degrees is 10% (answer c).

5. False. The percentage of Latinos who are living in poverty is lower than it was ten years ago.

6. False. Since 1994, violent crimes have decreased, reaching the lowest level ever recorded in 2005.

7. The percentage of murders in the United States that take place in schools is less than 1% (answer a). Students are safer at school than at home, work, or on the streets.

8. From 1994 to 2006, illicit drug use (other than marijuana) among twelfth-graders has decreased (answer c). In fact, 2006 saw the smallest percentage of students engaging in illicit drug use (other than marijuana) in that entire period.

9. Twenty-three percent of students in the United States take at least one AP

exam, the highest in our nation's history (answer c).

10. The average SAT scores for incoming freshmen rose from 1283 to 1335, a 52-point jump.

11. Students today score about 14 points higher on IQ tests than their grand-parents did and about 7 points higher than their parents did (answer c). The number of students with IQs above 145 is now about 18 times greater than it was two generations ago.

At a time when there is so much pressure to focus on test preparation and lower-level writing responses, the role of the research paper has diminished in public high schools. Yet, it is probably one of the most essential writing formats for all students to learn, especially underrepresented students. This is because adolescents, especially adolescents of color, are much maligned by the media. As I write this, the news of Cho Seung-Hu killing 32 students at Virginia Tech has set off a firestorm of commentary by talk radio hosts, news-paper columnists, and television personalities. Like in the aftermath of the shootings at Columbine in the 1990s, the media will brand students as violent and dangerous, and the notion that this current generation is somehow worse than past generations will be reinforced.

That is why teaching research writing is so critical. The only way to truly pierce the gauze of media distortion is to reveal the hard evidence on a given topic. Popular culture focuses so much on the sensational and the horrific that our perceptions—and our students' perceptions—too often are influenced by the extremes rather than the norms. This is why most students think that their generation is more violent (not true), more addicted to drugs (not true), more prone to teenage pregnancy and abortion (not true), and less successful in school (not true; indeed, quite the opposite is true). Every time I have students take the preceding quiz, they are amazed at how different their perceptions are from the image offered up by our media.

For underrepresented students, it is even worse. Students of color too often find that the media groups them in with the less desirable elements of our society, the caricatures and stereotypes reinforced by the talking heads on cable news shows who distort the truth to fit their particular ideology. The

101

best way to counter this mental programming is by equipping students with the tools to research and to think about information in a critical manner.

Coverage of teenage homicide on the evening news increased by 721 percent during the 1990s, even though the homicide rate decreased by about 20 percent in the same time frame (Schiraldi 1999). At the same time, when surveyed, people placed crime at the top of their list of fears. The principle here is clear: our perceptions are shaped by what we see rather than by facts. Also, most Americans, including adolescents, do not know the facts about the current generation. Mike Males, a longtime champion of adolescents, writes the following:

> The term "youth violence," a media and official staple, is inherently prejudicial. To understand this, consider how we treat other demographic groups. Example: About one million Orthodox Jews live in the United States. Crime statistics aren't kept by creed, but assume a half-dozen commit murder every year.
>
> This would give Orthodox Jews one of the lowest homicide rates of any group— probably the case. That means that every two months, on average, an Orthodox Jew is arrested for murder. Let's further assume that powerful political demagogues want to depict Jews as the font of violence, and the major media and institutions, as always, go along. Every couple of months, then, the press erupts, headlining "another Jew violence" tragedy, with sensational pictures and over-wrought speculation as to "why Jews are so violent." The press and politicians resolutely ignore thousands of intervening murders by non-Jews, including murders of Jews by Gentiles, while connecting every Jewish homicide, no matter how occasional, into a "spate of Jew killings." Conservatives angrily demand tougher policing of Jews. Liberals blame violent Jewish cultural messages. Politicians and private institutions form a National Campaign to Prevent Jew Violence.
>
> We need not add the seig-heils to realize that equating Jews and violence isn't an expression of science or genuine concern, but rank anti-Semitism. Linking an entire population class with a negative behavior practiced by only a few of its members is bigotry, regardless of which group is singled out. The politician-media-institution campaign on "youth violence" is bigoted and devoid of genuine concern for youths. Real concern would involve lamenting the major causes of violence against youths, yet politicians and institutions deploring "school violence" and pushing the National Campaign to Prevent Youth

> Violence concern themselves only with the tiny fraction of murdered children and youth that is politically advantageous to highlight while downplaying larger dangers to the young. (Males 2000)

For the most part, my students have grown up bombarded by messages that their generation is somehow inferior in morals and intellect to past generations. Another subtler message has been passed on to underrepresented students, which increases this idea of inferiority. To counter this, my introduction to research in the classroom begins with focusing students on a topic they are inherently interested in: themselves.

Reading Functional/Informational Text

The first day back from Spring Break, I place the chart shown in Figure 5.1 on the ELMO.

Figure 5.1 Passing Rates for the California High School Exit Examination (CAHSEE)

March and May 2001

Group	Percentage Passing Language Arts	Percentage Passing Math
All Students	64	44
Male	57.5	45.8
Female	71	43.1
Black/African American	49.6	24.3
Asian/Asian American	76.3	70.2
Hispanic/Latino	47.9	25.2
White (not of Hispanic origin)	81.5	63.6
English Learner	29.9	16.6
Special Education	22.8	12.8
Economically Disadvantaged	45.4	25.7

(California Department of Education)

At first, I let them see only the title, then I start them off by asking, "What is the topic of the chart and how is the chart structured?" These two questions will become the first two steps that we will take with every bit of research we do. Students quickly respond that the chart shows how many students have passed the Exit Exam in 2001. The chart has students divided up into different groups: gender, ethnicity, and special categories. In the past I have noticed that most students will want to just jump straight to the numbers without figuring out what they are looking at. If we want students to approach informational text with a critical mind, it is essential that they establish the precise topic and the type of structure that they are looking at.

The next step is to begin to work on comprehending the chart: what does it say? I ask students what they notice about the chart, then follow with questions to get them to think about the information they are processing. This year's conversation went something like this:

TURNER: What do you notice?

DESTINY: Latinos have the lowest pass rate in Language Arts.

TURNER: What would be a question an intelligent researcher would ask when confronted with that information?

SEVERAL STUDENTS: Why?

TURNER: What might be some possibilities? What further research might we do?

DESTINY: I'd like to know how many of those Latinos didn't speak English. How did just the English-speaking Latinos do on the exam?

TURNER: That's a great question.

We continue like this, discussing the role of poverty, gender, and other related issues. After about seven minutes of dissecting the chart, and questioning its contents, the students are ready to move on. We continue the same pattern of asking questions with each bit of informational text we look at:

- What is the topic? How is the chart structured?
- What does the chart say? What conclusions can we make?
- Why? What further research could we do?

Practice with Informational Text

At the end of the classroom discussion of *Romeo and Juliet*, we spent some time examining the differences between the two title characters. Juliet is certainly the stronger of the two, with Romeo being called "womanish" and "a baby" several times throughout the play. I pose the question, "Why would someone like Juliet choose someone like Romeo to be her husband?"

There are a host of reasons, all of which have some validity. But the one contributing factor that I like to explore is that Juliet, quite simply, wanted to get out of her parents' control. When someone in the class raises this possibility, I ask, "Do girls still do things like this today? Get married to get out of the house?" "Of course they do," the class replies. My follow-up is, "What else do teenagers sometimes do to get out of the control of their parents?" The answers this year include the following:

- Drugs
- Run away
- Join gangs
- Join the military
- Go to college
- Get a job
- Drop out of school
- Become super-involved at school
- Become pregnant
- Commit a crime/go to prison

This question frames the parameters of their first persuasive research paper. Over the course of the next few days, we will examine various nonfiction and informational texts, always approaching them with a critical, questioning mind. In pairs, students read the charts and text of Figure 5.2a and 5.2b, marking them up with questions, challenges, and avenues for further research.

Figure 5.2a

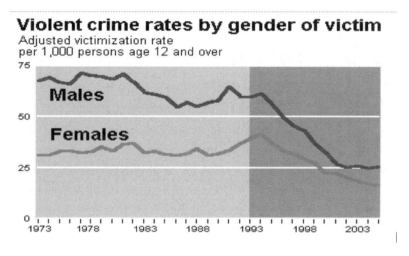

Figure 5.2b

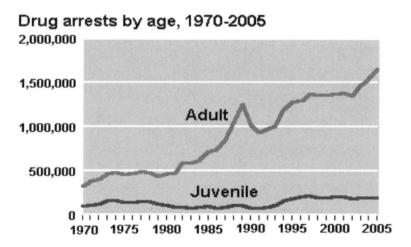

(United States Bureau of Justice Statistics. "Key Crime and Justice Stats at a Glance.")

My writers are asked to consider how the two charts relate to each other; good research skills include the ability to synthesize various bits of information.

After giving the students about five minutes to discuss the charts in pairs, we share our insights as a class and move on. Students repeat the process with the two charts shown in Chapter One of this book. I repeat this process a few times just to get them used to thinking critically about research—my goal here is to avoid having students simply swallow statistics, so we question and challenge informational texts, extrapolate on the possible ramifications of data, and most important, consider other areas of follow-up research.

Logical Fallacies and Informational Text

We want students to read informational and nonfiction texts with a discerning eye, which means that they need to be aware of the logical fallacies that are employed by those wishing to promote ideology rather than truth. Here are a few of my favorites:

FALSE CAUSE/POST HOC REASONING

When two events have a chronological relationship, and we assume there to be a causal relationship, we are guilty of the false cause logical fallacy. For instance, in the 1990s, President Clinton put thousands more police on the streets, and the crime rate went down. Naturally, many people said that *because* of the increase in police, the crime rate dropped. However, the crime rate was already dropping before the increase, the economy was on the rebound, and government-funded job training had once again become attainable. One would be short-sighted to make the claim that the reduced crime rate was due entirely to the increased police force.

Just because it rains every time I wash my car does not mean that washing my car makes it rain; it just feels that way.

HASTY GENERALIZATION

When we make an assumption about society based on a population sample that is too small to be accurate, we are guilty of a hasty generalization. For instance, just because a particular school sees an increase in test scores after initiating a particular program does not mean that the program is necessarily effective; to be accurate, we would need to see the same technique applied at various schools to see if the results are consistent.

FALSE DILEMMA

This is exemplified when a person constructs an argument giving his or her audience only two choices, usually one completely unacceptable alternative versus the preferred choice. One example of this is when students argue that marijuana should be legalized because it is not as harmful as alcohol.

FAULTY JUDGMENT

Kind of a catchall logical fallacy, this occurs when the conclusion one comes to just does not make sense based on the evidence.

STRAW MAN

When we reduce the opposition's argument into a caricature that is so ridiculous, no one would ever be swayed by it, we are guilty of creating a straw man. For instance, someone who argues that gun-control freaks want to take all the guns away and let only the criminals have firearms or someone who argues that the NRA wants to see every man, woman, and toddler armed with an AK-47: both of these are ridiculous assertions that distort the viewpoints of the two sides.

After going over these five logical fallacies, I give students a couple more charts and informational text to analyze. See if you can spot the problems with the chart and extract in Figure 5.3.

In the chart we have a sample size that is way too small: one school district cannot speak for a nation; therefore, the writers are guilty of a hasty generalization.

Figure 5.3 Chart and Informational Text for Logical Fallacy Analysis

From *Millennials Rising: The Next Great Generation* by Neil Howe and William Strauss (2000, 145):

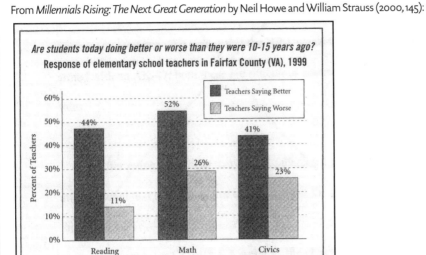

From *Dumbing Down Our Kids* by Charles J. Sykes (1996):
The result is a tragic legacy of educational mediocrity . . . SAT verbal scores have dropped from
a mean of 478 in 1962 to 423 in 1994, which is a drop of 54 points. The SAT mean math score has
fallen from 502 to 479, a drop of 23 points.([22])

In the text from *Dumbing Down Our Kids* (Sykes 1996), there is a problem
with the conclusion: more kids taking the SAT would naturally create a decrease
in the scores. There was a time when only elite students took the SAT, but as
more mainstream students apply to college, it is natural to see a drop in the
average score; thus, the writer is guilty of faulty judgment here.

To be honest, I am less concerned about the abilities of ninth graders to
use the terms I present than I am that they learn how to critically examine the
information they are presented with. With the advent of the Internet, anyone
can assert anything, and it will be swallowed whole by millions of unsuspecting
Googlers (at least that's what I read on Wikipedia).

Therefore, this exercise is a critical one in preparing students to research their own topics and logically examine the evidence without letting their own predispositions drive their conclusions.

Time to Research

We have spent nearly a week playing with various pieces of informational text that I have introduced to my students. I have asked them to choose a topic that they are interested in that is related to things teenagers do to escape the control of their parents. My writers have each chosen a topic and then a working thesis.

It is now time for my Puente students to do their research. Since research is a messy, time-consuming affair, I have to relinquish some control for the next couple of days. To keep the class on task as they research, I have them fill out a reflection sheet at the beginning and end of each class. This keeps me informed on how my students are doing, but more important, it helps them to set goals and use their time wisely. An example from a student is shown in Figure 5.4.

Figure 5.4 Research Reflection Sheet

Carina

Reflection Sheets

Beginning of Period:
I am currently at the
- [ ] Researching
- [x] Prewriting
- [ ] Drafting
- [ ] Sharing
- [ ] Revising
- [ ] editing

stage of writing the 2nd section.

What I need to accomplish today during class is:
Begin drafting section 2 or have an outline of what will be in section 2.

End of Period:
I am now at the
- [ ] Researching
- [ ] Prewriting
- [x] Drafting
- [ ] Sharing
- [ ] Revising
- [ ] editing

stage of writing the 2nd section.

What I accomplished today is:
I made the outline of what my 2nd section would look like and started drafting an intro to 2nd section

What I need to accomplish tonight for homework is:
2nd section

MLA Style

I present the details of MLA style pretty early in the writing process. In the past, I would wait until the end and then shudder because students had no idea that they were supposed to keep track of all the necessary information as they were researching.

The whole purpose behind documenting their sources, I explain, is that they alone do not have a lot of credibility yet—they lack a degree, they have never been published, etc. Therefore, they need to use the credibility of established sources to bolster their arguments, and probably the most common format to follow is based on the directions of the Modern Language Association (MLA). There are some specific rules that are laid forth by the MLA, and students need to follow them as they write.

I place the following document on the ELMO:

DOCUMENTING SOURCES

1. A lot of teenagers watch too much television.
2. Dr. Finkelstein says a lot of teenagers watch too much television.
3. Dr. Finkelstein, a psychologist who specializes in adolescent behavior, states "a lot of teenagers watch too much television."
4. Dr. Finkelstein, a psychologist who specializes in adolescent behavior, states in the May 1998 issue of *Medical Journal,* "a lot of teenagers watch too much television."
5. Dr. Finkelstein, a psychologist who specializes in adolescent behavior, states in the May 1998 issue of *Medical Journal,* "a lot of teenagers watch too much television," which quite possibly explains the drop in scholastic achievement and the increase in dropout rates. He goes on to state that the "number one effect of watching more than five hours a day of TV is an increased tendency toward violent behavior," which is yet another negative consequence of allowing teenagers to have free rein over the television set (17).

First the writing itself. In the last example, the writer has accomplished the following:

- Established credibility by announcing a significant source, including the place and date of the quoted material

- Successfully integrated quoted material with the writer's own words
- Blended research with the writer's own opinions and commentary

Second, the in-text documentation. When writers use words or ideas from a credible source, the MLA asks them to include some information at the end of the sentence or passage (if it is not stated directly in the text itself). Specifically, the MLA asks for the author's last name and the page number on which the reference material appears. However, this information is not always available— sometimes, writers use a source with no stated author, in which case they need to follow the hierarchy set forth by MLA. I write the following on the board and have my students copy it into their writer's notebooks:

(Author's Last Name #)

▼

(Name of Text #)

▼

(Name of Website)

▼

(URL)

If the author's name is not available, students should write the name of the text and the page number in parentheses; if that's not available, then the name of the website and so on. After explaining this, I place my students in groups to practice both in-text documentation and the creation of a mock work's cited page:

PRACTICE IN-TEXT DOCUMENTATION

Please write the following statements, correctly documenting your sources.

1. The death penalty has proven to be ineffective at curbing kidnapping, as child abduction rates have "gone through the roof" over the past several years.

   —the information was taken from Art Brush's Pulitzer Prize–winning article, "The New Wave of Kidnappers" from *Time* magazine, published on April 20, 2003. The article is found on pages 34–47; the specific quotation is found on page 37.

2. Oddly enough, most students who purchase their lunch in school rather than bring a lunch from home are "20% more likely to suffer from a learning disability and 35% more likely to earn low grades."

—the information was taken from Jim Nasium's textbook, *The Effects of Cafeteria Food on America's Youth*. From Penguin Publishers, published in 2003 in New York City. The book is 347 pages long; the specific quotation is found on page 317. It was illustrated by Jim Bernardin.

3. As Attorney General Alberto Gonzales has stated, "no laws were broken in the implementation of this policy."

—the information was taken from an editorial in *The New York Times*, "A Defense of Karl Rove," published in November 2005. No author is listed. The article is found on pages A13–A47; the specific quotation is found on page A17.

4. As Matt Shtick, an FDNY chief has argued, "arson remains one of our gravest threats in society today."

—the information was taken from Shtick's article "Protecting Ourselves From Arson" from *The Los Angeles Times* newspaper, published in 2002. The article is found on pages A4–7; the specific quotation is found on page A5.

5. Motivational expert and author Gladys Seeyaw has joined the chorus of those asking for less medication abuse in society, claiming that it "has really gotten out of hand in modern society."

—the information was taken from a website called *Hugs Not Drugs for Thugs with Hairplugs*. It was posted on November 3, 2006, and is produced by the DARE program. The information is found at hugsnotdrugsforthugswithhairplugs.com. You found the information on November 11, 2007. When you print out the information, it is seventeen pages long.

6. According to one source, "dyslexia seems to be more commonplace with this new generation."

—the information was taken from a personal interview conducted in 2006 with Ron Deeyemsee.

In my seven years of teaching freshman composition at Fullerton College, I've noticed that some writers either simply parrot research (data dumping) without including their own opinions or they offer unsupported commentary without research to back themselves up. I try to counter this in my high school class by having my writers consider how they are going to use each piece of research in their own argument; their ideas, supported by research, should drive their papers. Therefore, as students begin their research, I instruct them to jot down four basic blocks of information for every source they use: the URL (or call number), the information being quoted or paraphrased, their commentary, and the necessary documentation information. As they research, I walk around the room checking their research sheets containing this information and answering questions.

Drafting the Research Paper

Writing an argument research paper is difficult. Many students fall into one of two traps: either they want to pontificate without research to support themselves or they simply parrot the research that is out there, a technique some of my colleagues have referred to as "data dumping." Either one is bad. A good argument research paper will have a nice balance between the two, offering about twice as much of the writer's thinking as the research that backs it up.

At the beginning of the drafting process, I hand my students a copy of a paragraph from a previous student's paper and a pair of highlighters. They are instructed to highlight all research in blue and all the writer's thoughts or commentary in pink. In the example that follows, the boldface type is the writer's own thinking, and the underlined text is research.

For a century now, the world has been involved in debate over capital punishment, and in order to understand why, we must examine the very components of such a structure, unraveling its pattern until we can see each individual thread for what it is. The easiest thread to pick at would be its effectiveness as a deterrent within society. There is no solid evidence in existence that the death penalty is useful as a deterrent or that

it decreases crime, and so agrees former Attorney General Janet Reno, stating, "I have inquired for most of my adult life about studies that might show that the death penalty is a deterrent. And I have not seen any research that would substantiate that point" (*The Nation*). **Many states have decided to pump their money into prisons as opposed to educational systems, an appalling fact when considering the grotesque amount of money that is wasted on punishment by execution.** Sending a guilty party to death row costs an average of $2.3 million, three times the amount of solitary confinement at the highest security level for forty years. Florida has spent more than $53 million a year, $90 million in California (Bender), more on state executions than it would have spent on punishing all first-degree murderers with life in prison without parole (Jackson). **Eliminating the death penalty within a state frees up funds that could be put to positive use. For example, instead of paying for state-sanctioned murder, rehabilitation or early educational programs could be developed. Education provides opportunity and opportunity in turn provides a path other than that of crime. Instead of waiting until a crime is already committed, the focus should be on preventing them in the first place.**

Through this exercise, I am attempting to train my students to balance their research with their own thinking, so that their papers are still driven by their own voices but are bolstered by the credible research supporting their thinking.

As students work through their first draft, I return to the concept of using research to strengthen their claims rather than simply reacting to research as many students are prone to do. Giving them the two sample paragraphs that follow, I ask them to discuss with a neighbor which one blends research with the writer's opinions more effectively.

Paragraph I

As Richard Grayson points out, "a significant amount of all automobile accidents occur because of cell phone usage" (35). This is so ridiculous. We shouldn't be using our cell phones when we drive unless it's an emergency, like our kids needing medical attention. When we drive, we should be focused on the road and other drivers. Lives are at stake.

Paragraph II

Although eating while driving has contributed to automobile accidents, it pales when compared to the effect of cell phones. We've become a nation addicted to our ubiquitous handheld phones, and they permeate everything we do—including driving. Unfortunately, they create unsafe driving conditions as "a significant amount of all automobile accidents occur because of cell phone usage" (Grayson 35), a statistic that ominously warns us that the future is grim. As Verizon and Cingular continue to expand, so, it seems, will the number of automobile accidents in the country.

Revising the Research Paper

We are now fast approaching May, or as it's known in California, The 31 Days of Testing (a slight exaggeration but not entirely inaccurate). I am feeling the pressure that comes with the limited number of days left for me to teach college-level writing habits to my students.

We have reviewed many of the skills learned earlier in the year—for some reason, students tend to disengage their writing abilities when they switch to this genre. I have dedicated time to writing engaging introductions, transitioning between ideas, establishing the credibility of sources, integrating quoted research, and using powerful verbs; I have also reinforced my teaching of documentation. However, when the first drafts come in to me, I am very disappointed and I pull a few samples to review with the class.

There are a few bright moments, however: Sara has made an amazing recovery after a brutal first semester, and Marco has turned around as well and is now on task nearly all the time. I try to stay focused on these while still reaching out to some of the struggling students.

Many of the students are now e-mailing me regularly with questions about their papers, which is an encouraging sign. I know that in college, student visits to professors during office hours is extremely important. After a few conferences and e-mail exchanges, Norma revises her paper on bullies and is ready to turn it in. Still rough, even for a freshman, the paper shows she is starting to get how to write an argument-based research paper.

BULLIES: PUNISHED OR HELPED

NORMA CHAVARIN

ENGLISH I

MR. TURNER

I turned 20 less than 15 days ago. I thought by now I would've forgotten about what happened to me in junior and high school ... They harassed me constantly every day that summer before high school. They'd call me on the phone and say the meanest things, making fun of my family and me both physically and personality wise ... I didn't want them saying things to my family the way they did to me, so I took it all ... Even though they did come to my house, I'd go outside and take their crap 'til they were finished ... I never told anybody this 'til I was 18. I didn't think anyone would care. Kids get bullied every day at school. The school doesn't care. Because of them I was miserable for five friggin' years. I wanted to die. I wanted the world to end. I wanted to kill (Michelle's Story).

Every day, bullies pick on victims and make them suffer. Their long suffering cuases them so much pain and their pain does not result into anything good. Typically, when a student does something wrong, they usually get punished, but does punishment help solve the nationwide problem?

According to the National Institutes of Child Help and Human Development (NICHD), 35% of the students in the United States are affected by bullying behavior, and out of those people, "16% say they have been bullied, 13% say they have bullied others, and 6% say they have been bullied and bullied others," (3) concluding that there are more victims of bullies than there are bullies. Therefore, bullying has become a nationwide problem that needs attention. For this reason, "bullying makes children's lives a misery and must be punished" (Carnell). The majority of victims are vulnerable and scared of bullies, which is why approximately, "160,000 students a day miss school 'for fear of being picked on'" (Nevius), mostly because they have low self-esteem and don't confide in anyone to tell them their problems. In fact, it wasn't until the author of "Michelle's Story" was eighteen years old that she had enough confidence in others to tell anyone what happened to her in junior and high school because she "didn't think anyone would care." She felt scared because she couldn't really stand up for herself.

In very few, rare cases, bullying can be so serious that the victims can't take the ongoing suffering, and as a result, they take their own lives. Tom Trosvik was one of the victims of bullies who decided that taking his life away would be the best solution:

Why, they thought, would a 12-year-old boy take his own life? They would later learn the bullying was worse than originally thought. "It was on the school bus that he [was] being picked on, and the kids were actually teasing him on how he would go out and kill himself in different ways" (Fryer).

Tom was just one of the few victims of bullying that ended up committing suicide. He was vulnerable, just like Michelle. He didn't have the confidence to tell a reliable adult to confide. For these reasons, many people feel that the deaths and victims of bullies must be avenged. The bullies need a taste of their own medicine, some argue, in order for them to stop, or how else would they learn?

Some forms of punishment do exist—although not severe—in the United States. Currently in Houston, Texas, the punishment "for a student who bullied or verbally abused another student to have a report sent home to parents and a possibility of a detention" (HISD Wants To Crack Down"). The district is now realizing that bullying is a major issue and for that reason, a person who assaults another student "whether or not bodily injury is involved requires removal to a disciplinary alternative school" (ibid).

Despite the bullies being bad guys, trying to at least forgive them would do them good. In fact, that's exactly what God wants everyone to do. He wants everyone to "be kind to one another, compassionate, forgiving one another as God has forgiven [us]" (Eph 4:32). God does not want humanity to be full of hatred, anger, or revenge. Therefore, having hate and punishing others for their actions would not solve a thing, and in fact, makes matters worse. Even if it weren't in the Bible, punishment is not always the most effective method to solve any ongoing problem. Based on research done by Dr. Belinda Hopkins, "punishment makes a person resentful, not reflective . . . and does not provide the perpetrator with an opportunity to repair harm" (3) that is already present. Punishment will not always make a difference to all bullies until they "face up to the reality of just how many people have been affected directly and indirectly by their behavior" (3), which hopefully can open the eyes of the bullies and encourage a call for action.

Alternatives for punishment can consist of programs that can help bullies learn to accept their problem and find a solution. First of all, According to Stan Davis of the International Bullying Prevention Association, bullies need to learn how to do the following:

- Acknowledge their own actions
- Acknowledge results of their behavior on themselves
- Develop anxiety
- Change actions (for the future)
- Find other ways to get their needs met
- Acknowledge behavior toward others
- Develop guilt
- Learn to trust others
- Form relationships with helping adults

Once they have done so, they are ready to avoid future bullying behavior and begin to realize that they have harmed many innocent people. There are programs that are dedicated to helping bullies and victims go through processes that can stop, prevent, and deal with bullying. For instance, the Olweus family founded one of the successful programs, administered to many schools, such as Chula Vista High School. Chula Vista has been "recognized with a 2005 Helen Putnam Award from league of CA cities," and for adopting nine other schools into this program.

Bullies should be offered another opportunity to start over. After all, they are human. They make mistakes just like the rest of mankind. Society needs to feel empathy toward bullies because sometimes the reasons why bullies engage in negative behavior make them seem like victims. For example, bullies feel the need to display their emotions, which is sometimes caused by the lack of "warmth and parental attention" (Davis); because they feel so lonely, they find a loner at school and taunt him or her until they feels like the victim is traumatized. In other cases, the bullies experience "physical punishment" (Davis) from their parents, causing them in turn to hurt other individuals. Bullies, too, face difficulties in their lives and sadly, they result into hurting others in return.

Despite the fact that bullies leave numerous victims traumatized throughout their lives and some of their victims even commit suicide, bullies should not be given punishment, but instead, should be offered help. Although bullying often seems common part of growing up, it actually "is not just an unpleasant rite of passage through childhood. It's a public health problem that merits attention" (Alexander). Helping bullies realize their wrongdoings would be a small but important step in reducing the bullying rates in the United States.

Works Cited

Alexander, Dr. Duane. 24 Apr 2001. National Institute of Child Health. 2 Apr 2007.
   http://www.yellodyno.com/html/bullying_stats.html.

Alvarez, Dr. Manny. "Zero Tolerance for Bullies." 16 Apr 2007. Fox Fan Central. 7 May
   2007. http://www.foxnews.com/story/0,2933,182171,00.html.

Carnell, Liz. "Schools." 1999. Bullying Online. 7 May 2007. http://www.bullying.co.uk/
   schools/dealinwithbullies.php.

Davis, Stan. International Bullying Prevention Association. 27 Apr 2007. http://www.
   stopbullyingnow.com/interven2.htm.

"HISD Wants to Crack Down on Bullying, Cheating." 6 Jun 2006. Click2Houston. 7 May
   2007. http://www.click2houston.com/news/927917/detail.html.

Fryer, Joe. "Bullying Gone Too Far." 3 May 2007. Kare 11 News. 7 May 2007. http://www.
   karell.com/news_article.aspx?storyid=252388.

Hopkins, Dr. Belinda. "National Centre for Restorative Justice in Education." Jan 2006.
   7 May 2007. http://www.transformingconflict.org/Nov%202006%20Bullying%20
   article.doc.

Michelle. "Michelles Story." 17 Apr 2001. *Raven Days.* 7 May 2007. http://www.
   ravendays.org/words/michelle.html.

Nevius, C.W. "The National Association of School Psychologists." 5 Oct 2003. Hearst
   Communications. 7 May 2007. http://www.sfgate.com/cgi-bin/article.cgi?f=/
   c/a/2003/10/05/LVI7087.DTL.

The International Student Bible for Catholics: New American Bible. Nashville. Thomas
   Nelson Publishers, 1999.

The University Paper

Students require multiple opportunities to work with research-based argument pieces. Although I introduce the genre in ninth grade, the cementing of the skills required to write such a paper really takes place in tenth grade. One of the opportunities for students to hone their craft in writing research papers will take place with the university research paper, a quick exploration of possible colleges for my writers. We usually do this paper just before our three-day tour of California universities. To begin, students are asked to research schools that they might consider attending, and then to research those schools using the research sheets. Many of my students worry about being rejected by a prestigious university; one of the first steps here is to get them to shift their thinking so that they realize that in fact they are consumers of education, and these schools are selling them opportunities to study on their campuses. At this stage of their education, students need to think of themselves as shopping for a college with as much preparation as one would take in buying a car, or house, or selecting a mate. It will be the single largest decision they have made yet. Also, it helps students think through the next several years and carefully consider what they need to accomplish in order to attend the school of their choice.

After a student of mine was accepted to Berkeley without ever having seen the campus or the town, I began dedicating two weeks to the research and writing of this small paper. Creating a college-going culture on my campus requires students to spend time learning about their options. Here is the prompt for the paper my students write their sophomore year:

UNIVERSITY RESEARCH PAPER

Choose a few universities (2–4) that you're considering attending. After much research, write a paper in which you argue which of the universities would be best for you AND what you have done/will need to do in order to attend this school. Consider discussing any/all of the following:
- Location / environment
- Unique characteristics
- Diversity
- Sports / clubs
- Majors offered / programs the school is known for
- Cost
- Requirements to get in (include GPA, SAT scores, etc.)
- Type of school—UC, CSU, private, etc.
- What external sources (i.e., not the school itself) say about the university
- Any other appealing feature of the school

You'll want to begin the paper with an introduction that engages the reader and guides your audience toward your thesis; end the paper with a conclusion that leaves the reader thinking about your thesis.

College Research Data Sheets

To help their research, the students fill in the data sheet reprinted in Figure 5.5, focusing on those categories that truly matter to them. A blank, full-page version of this sheet is in Appendix C.

Figure 5.5 Sample College Research Data Sheet

College Research Data Sheet

1. General Information

School name _UC Davis_ Source used _www.ucdavis.edu_

Phone _(503) 752-2971_ Type of School _UC_ Semester/Quarter _Quarter_

Location _Davis, near Sacramento_

2. Demographic Information

Student body size/undergrads (# of freshmen) _23,018 (4,268)_

Setting _suburban, small city_ %Women /% Men _58/42_ Students w/ 3.0+ GPA _98%_

% Students in top 10th of class: _95%_ Top quarter: _100%_ Top half: _100%_

SAT middle 50% of first-year students: Math _550-660_ Verbal _490-620_

Ethnic Breakdown (top 5 ethnicities, % of student body):

1. _43% Asian / Pacific Islander_
2. _33% White_
3. _12% Hispanic_
4. _8% Unreported_
5. _3% Black_

% in fraternities _____ % in sororities _____

3. Program Information

Special study options that appeal to you _Study Abroad, Washington Seminar_

Sports that appeal to you _N/A_

AP policy _Offers credit + placement into higher classes for successful AP Exams_

Majors that appeal to you _Biology and Engineering_

Activities available _Radio Station_

4. Admission Factors

Summarize what admission factors are considered _Essays, SAT, Subject Tests, Rigor of Classes, Standardized Test Scores, Class Rank, Extracurricular Activities, Personal Qualities._

Sample University Paper

Once the research has been done, students take their papers through the writing process, focusing on a particular school that they would seriously consider attending. After writing the body of the paper, students work on engaging introductions. Once finished, we take a day to read choice passages from their papers.

UC BERKELEY RESEARCH PAPER

GRISELDA GUTIERREZ

PERIOD ONE

MR. TURNER

There she was. Sitting at the dinner table. She seemed transfixed upon her work. Next to her were what seemed like hills and hills of papers and books. After a few months, this all became monotonous, yet I did not understand why she would stay up past midnight doing a vast amount of work. At this time, I was in eighth grade and it all seemed so simple to me. I would spend two hours a day doing homework and studying and soon after would run off with my friends to do things that seemed more important at this time. A couple of months later, I understood that all of this hard work had paid off for her: she had been accepted to the University of California in Berkeley. I also understood that two hours of studying and doing homework would not be enough in order to achieve what my sister has achieved. It was then that I decided to follow in her footsteps and go on to a prestigious university. Since then I have used my sister's accomplishments as motivation toward my goal of attending a four-year university. Because of my realization of how important college is, I intend on attending the University of California in Berkeley as well.

In order to achieve my goal of becoming a Berkeley student, I acknowledge the fact that not only will I need good S.A.T. scores and a high grade point average, but extracurricular activities as well. These are important factors that I have to take under consideration when accomplishing my goal. According to the Director of Undergraduate Admissions at U.C. Berkeley, they are "looking for students that have leadership and an interest in activities," and they "look at applicants beyond grade point average and S.A.T. scores" (U.C. Berkeley). Therefore, not only will I have to work hard and study, I will also have to join many leadership programs. By doing so, I will become more of a well-rounded student and will meet more of the requirements needed to get accepted into Berkeley.

Furthermore, the reasons for my first choice in a university being Berkeley are because of its location, and because of its majors. Because it's located in a city near the excitement of San Francisco and Oakland, it has become more appealing to me. Since most of my time will be spent studying and doing homework, I want to be able to use any extra time to go out and do something other than to study. Berkeley is the preferred school for me because I can do both: study and socialize.

Also at this university, there are over one hundred majors, and a noted School of Business and a renown College of Engineering (Gutierrez). Since I am interested in majoring in engineering or business, I have chosen Berkeley as the place to study.

Even though most of the students that attend Berkeley are Asian and white (Gutierrez), that does not deter me from attending. The fact that I might be one of a few Latinas that attend this school does not have much of an impact on my decision. I am prepared to be a minority at Berkeley.

After getting accepted, there are other important aspects that go along with studying at the school, such as its cost. It is important because the school costs about twenty-thousand a semester. Ten thousand of this is for room and board (Financial Aid Office). Therefore, this is going to be something of great importance once I get accepted to U.C. Berkeley. Although cost is important, there are many ways to get money for school, and money shouldn't be a problem (Gutierrez). Therefore, I should not base my decision mainly on how I will pay for my schooling, because I can always find a way.

If I get accepted to Berkeley, I have to find a place to live located near the school. There are many dorms near the school where I can live once I am already attending the university. For example, there are three main dorms near the school, consisting of the Griffiths, Davidson, and Cunningham Halls, each housing about two hundred and fifty students (Unit Two Residence).

Starting this year, I will study for the S.A.T.s that will take place in May of my junior year. This will help me prepare for them and will improve my scores on the verbal and in the math section because the average S.A.T. scores required for Berkeley range from 570–700 on the verbal section and 670–740 in math (U.C. Berkeley). By studying from now until May, I will not have to stress out about doing poorly on them. Not only will I have to study for my S.A.T.s, but I will also study and work hard in all of my classes in order to keep a high grade point average. The average unweighted grade point average is 3.84 and the weighted one is 4.24 (U.C. Berkeley). Since the average grade point averages needed are high, I will have to be dedicated to my work in order to meet these requirements.

Throughout these two years that I have been in high school, I have been in a program known as Puente, which has and will continue to prepare me for a four year university. This program will help me get into a four-year university and will also look good on my college applications. This year I have also joined a program called CSF, and during the next two years, I will enroll in many Advanced Placement classes that will count as credit toward college. For example, next year I will have five AP classes, all which will look great on my college applications. Not only will I have to take more rigorous classes, but I will also join many leadership programs in order to get into Berkeley. This year I have joined the Puente Cabinet, in which we discuss activities that will take place at Magnolia High School, and we are also able to share our ideas for events that we want to see take place. I will continue to exhibit leadership and take advantage of all the opportunities presented to me, which in turn will help my chances of being accepted to Berkeley (U.C. Berkeley). Therefore, I will do as much as possible throughout these next two years in order for my chances of getting accepted into U.C. Berkeley to be greater.

Community service is one of the most important factors when applying to a prestigious university. These schools look at a student's activities and also want to make sure that they've taken advantage of their opportunities (U.C. Berkeley). During my two years in high school, I have done community service and volunteer work. For thanksgiving, I was present at the Casa Garcia restaurant with students from other schools. There, we helped out with food which was given to those who are less fortunate. During the weekend, I sometimes also help out at the YMCA. There, I help out my brother-in-law wash out vans and clean some of the classrooms. By continuing to do this throughout my time left in high school, my chances of getting into a four-year university will be greater.

The next couple of years in high school will be the most important years of my life. This is when I have to do as much as possible in order for me to make it into U.C. Berkeley. By providing leadership and joining many clubs, I will have more chances of getting accepted. By doing this and more, I will have achieved my goal of getting into a prestigious university and following in my sister's footsteps.

Works Cited

"Financial Aid Office." U.C. Berkeley website. 3 Mar 2004. www.berkeley.edu.

Gutierrez, Gabriela. Personal Interview. 19 Mar 2004.

"Scholarship Prizes Honors." 3 Mar 2004. www.berkeley.edu.

U.C. Berkeley Residence Halls. www.reshall.berkeley.edu.

U.C. Berkeley Website. 3 Mar 2004. www.berkeley.edu.

Conclusion

The requirements for a student to succeed in college differ greatly from the scripted curriculum too often forced upon underrepresented students who attend under-performing high schools. No Child Left Behind has forced the secondary educational institutions in many poorer neighborhoods to concentrate solely on minimal-thinking skills that can be measured with multiple-choice simplicity, and it has caused those same institutions to ignore the higher-level thinking required in college. To graduate students who test satisfactorily for state measurements but lack entry-level college skills is unforgivable.

One of the highest goals we educators can reach for is to nurture in our students the ability to read multiple viewpoints and information, to make sense of them, and to synthesize them into their own positions that can then be argued with appropriate evidence. That is building an informed citizenry, and that is precisely what is so desperately needed in today's global climate.

Unfortunately, too often, this does not happen.

Students require multiple attempts at writing research-based arguments, and have to be allowed the freedom to practice such writing several times before they attain mastery. In my class, although students frequently work with evaluating the credibility of sources, I am realizing that they need more opportunities to do so if I want them to be competitive with other students at prestigious universities, and more important, to be able to filter the mental noise of bias and information manipulation. As an English teacher with high hopes for my students, I need to withstand the weight of test preparation that can eclipse authentic teaching, and instead teach my students how to distinguish between credible and non-credible sources, the skill of synthesizing several texts, and proficiency in shaping an argument by pulling appropriate evidence from those texts and using correct documentation. Those skills do not come cheaply or quickly, but to ignore them exacts an even greater price in the lives of our students.

CHAPTER SIX

Exploring Culture-Based Writing

In the previous chapters I have discussed autobiographical/biographical writing, literary analysis, and persuasive/research writing; all three are commonly taught (and tested) in high schools across the nation. This chapter focuses on a fourth type of writing that is centered on the community or culture to which a student belongs. The subject matter is usually overlooked, but it can be used as a powerful force in the classroom.

When the word *culture* is used, most think of race or ethnicity. However, a person is shaped by many cultures that reach far beyond solely race. Ethnographer Clifford Geertz, in describing culture, uses the metaphor of a web, where each strand represents a different factor in a person's identity: religion, income, geography, education, career, generation, and others (Geertz 1973). All these strands of culture form a very complex mechanism that greatly influences our actions and beliefs.

In other words, culture is not limited to ethnicity—there is a myriad of forces at play in our lives. For many underrepresented students, investigating those forces and researching them can be invigorating because there is just enough of the student involved to appeal to his or her egocentric self, and yet there is a great deal of analysis and research, which makes it a great academic exercise.

A person's economic class serves as an example of culture that transcends ethnicity. I grew up in a working-class neighborhood in Orange County called Garden Grove. In my neighborhood people worked on their cars in the driveway and lawns and shopped at discount stores, and many teenagers smoked. After eighth grade, my parents and I moved to Mission Viejo, a much more affluent area in the southern section of Orange County. There were rules against working on your car in the driveway, no discount stores existed, and smoking was generally looked down upon. Although in the late 1970s both neighborhoods were predominantly white, the cultures of the two neighborhoods were completely different.

The research and sharing of one's culture engages many otherwise disconnected students. For many students, it also transforms a perceived liability into a strength. Because of this built-in interest, I have made use of cultural writing in dealing with underrepresented students and have had much success.

Now, in the middle of May, I am eager to embark on culture-based writing. The students are acclimated to the constant writing and are beginning to truly see themselves as future university students. Carlos, a senior Puente student, has just been accepted to Stanford University, a feat that only two other students from Magnolia High School have ever achieved—both of them have also been Puente students. Frankie, another senior Puente student, has been accepted to UC Berkeley, and about three-quarters of the Puente class of 2007 is headed straight to a four-year university.

The freshmen know all of this, of course. They feel connected to the successes of these senior students, plugged into a *familia*, and many want to follow in the footsteps of Carlos and Frankie and the others. As a result, several students are transforming into much more serious students—Sara has been participating in discussions and staying on task during drafting time in class; Marco has been steadily bringing up his grades in his other classes and asking for help with his writing. The constant focus on my Puente students' eventual goal—the university—has propelled many to work toward straight A's in their classes. Destiny, my continuously smiling fountain of happiness;

Joanna, all business and solemnity during class work; Edgar, the soft-spoken academic leader; Johanna, the seemingly sweet band member who is ruthless to those who cross her; Ashley, the shy, always-proper sweetheart; Norma, who is increasingly attracted to the cultural aspects of the class and is in the process of discovering her identity as a Latina; and especially Armando, the cheerful, upbeat class representative who has emerged as a beloved class leader despite a crazy haircut that marks him as a freshman—they all are showing me progress reports with straight A's. Any of them could end up at the university of their dreams as long as the Puente team keeps their goals in front of them and develops them into leaders in their community rather than followers of the Magnolia High School adolescent culture, which too often influences some to take the easiest way through school. Therefore, it is time to begin getting my writers to examine their places in the communities they belong to and the subcultures they identify with.

My first step in getting students to think and write about culture is to have them read a reflective essay that appears in many college readers, "The Good Daughter." I usually begin by writing the word *culture* up on the board and then asking the class what comes to mind when I mention this word. After a short brainstorm, I reveal the title of the essay and ask students what they expect the piece to be about. Below is the first basic lesson that I follow; the rest of the chapter outlines the path I take in dealing with culture.

"The Good Daughter"

Caroline Hwang's "The Good Daughter" (1998) is my favorite piece of fiction to use in dealing with culture. I've included it in ninth-grade classes and college classes; it always sparks rich discussion and sets the stage for culture-based or community-based thinking and writing.

I usually begin by telling students the name of the essay prior to reading it, then asking, "What might this story be about?" Students will usually offer the title back to me, then very quickly deduce that it might be about someone who *isn't* a good daughter after all. A second question that I have asked on occasion is, "What would keep a daughter from being considered good?" which sets the students up to discuss cultural/community expectations.

Afterward, we read the first paragraph together out loud.

> The moment I walked into the dry-cleaning store, I knew the woman behind the counter was from Korea, like my parents. To show her that we shared a heritage, and possibly get a fellow countryman's discount, I tilted my head forward, in shy imitation of a traditional bow.

In pairs or groups of three, I give my students one minute to discuss everything they can deduce about this speaker from just this paragraph; then we share our ideas as a class. Students will usually claim that she's Korean, she's cheap, and she doesn't know much about being Korean. Other deductions will surface, but the class usually notes these three things before we move on to the next part of the essay:

> "Name?" she asked, not noticing my attempted obeisance.
> "Hwang," I answered.
> "Hwang? Are you Chinese?"
> Her question caught me off-guard. I was used to hearing such queries from non-Asians who think Asians all look alike, but never from one of my own people. Of course, the only Koreans I knew were my parents and their friends, people who've never asked me where I came from, since they knew better than I.

At this point, I give the class another minute to discuss what they are noticing. After sharing, I then give them a copy of the complete essay and a highlighter, and we finish reading the piece together. Students are instructed to highlight anything that stands out to them.

After reading the rest of "The Good Daughter," I place students in groups of five or six (combining the smaller groups in which they began the lesson) and ask them to share what they have highlighted and why they think it has stood out to them; then, I give them a couple of minutes to discuss the ways in which they think Hwang's culture affects her. While they are discussing this, I wander about the room, eavesdropping on the insights they are coming up with. When I feel as if most groups have engaged in a discussion about culture and the character's "in between" status, I am ready to bring them back into a large-group setting. After they have spent several minutes working through the text, the students share their ideas as a class. I usually ask a few follow-up questions as they share, but students respond to each other and do almost all of the talking; my only job is to ask questions:

Student Response	Follow-up Question
"The mom doesn't care if Hwang knows her culture."	*Why do you think it doesn't matter to the mom?*
"The main character seems white-washed."	*What does that term* (white-washed) *mean, exactly? How do we define it?*
"She's in between Korean culture and American culture."	*How common is that feeling of being "in between" among children of immigrants?*
"Her parents put unfair pressures on her."	*What exactly do her parents do that is unfair? What makes it unfair?*
"Her mom says that Hwang isn't Korean, that she's American."	*What does that phrase mean? Culturally, what does it mean to be American?*
"She seems cut off from Korean culture."	*What culture does she seem to identify most strongly with?*

That last question is an important one. For them to engage in culture or community-based writing, they have to understand that culture transcends ethnicity. In the essay, Hwang is facing multiple cultural expectations—strands on the spiderweb—and having trouble making them fit in her life.

In my experience, most students face similar conflicts—parents want them to be successfully assimilated in American society (after all, that's often the incentive for immigrating here to begin with) but not at the expense of their ethnic culture. Many of my students get caught up trying to follow the dictates of two or more cultures that sometimes conflict with each other.

For instance, I come from a fairly close-knit family that used to have frequent get-togethers throughout the year. Nearly every Sunday, in fact, my family would drive up to Compton, where my grandparents lived, and spend the afternoon with them. When I started college, however, that simply wasn't possible for me. Between working full-time to pay for my schooling and the amount of reading and writing we English majors were expected to do, I simply could not sacrifice an entire day very often.

That did not go over so well with my family; although they wanted me to succeed academically, they did not want me to miss out on our family time. The cultural conflict that I experienced is magnified in my students' lives. Underrepresented students nearly always straddle the worlds of academia and family; it has to do with more than just ethnicity. Being the first in your family to go on to college often causes this friction.

I share my background with my students at the conclusion of Hwang's essay. For homework, I ask them to make a list of several cultures or communities they see themselves belonging to.

The Good Daughter
by Caroline Hwang

The moment I walked into the dry-cleaning store, I knew the woman behind the counter was from Korea, like my parents. To show her that we shared a heritage, and possibly get a fellow countryman's discount, I tilted my head forward, in shy imitation of a traditional bow.

"Name?" she asked, not noticing my attempted obeisance.

"Hwang," I answered.

"Hwang? Are you Chinese?"

Her question caught me off-guard. I was used to hearing such queries from non-Asians who think Asians all look alike, but never from one of my own people. Of course, the only Koreans I knew were my parents and their friends, people who've never asked me where I came from, since they knew better than I.

I ransacked my mind for the Korean words that would tell her who I was. It's always struck me as funny (in a mirthless sort of way) that I can more readily say "I am Korean" in Spanish, German and even Latin than I can in the language of my ancestry. In the end, I told her in English.

The dry-cleaning woman squinted as though trying to see past the glare of my strangeness, repeating my surname under her breath. "Oh, Fxuang," she said, doubling over with laughter. "You don't know how to speak your name."

I flinched. Perhaps I was particularly sensitive at the time, having just dropped out of graduate schoool. I had torn up my map for the future, the one that said not only where I was going but who I was. My sense of identity was already disintegrating.

When I got home, I called my parents to ask why they had never bothered to correct me. "Big deal," my mother said, sounding more flippant than I knew she intended. (Like many people who learn English in a classroom, she uses idioms that don't always fit the occasion.) "So what if you can't pronounce your name? You are American," she said.

Though I didn't challenge her explanation, it left me unsatisfied. The fact is, my cultural identity is hardly that clear-cut.

My parents immigrated to this country 30 years ago, two years before I was born. They told me often, while I was growing up, that, if I wanted to, I could be president someday, that here my grasp would be as long as my reach.

To ensure that I reaped all the advantages of this country, my parents saw to it that I became fully assimilated. So, like any American of my generation, I whiled away my youth strolling malls and talking on the phone, rhapsodizing over Andrew McCarthy's blue eyes or analyzing the meaning of a certain upperclassman's offer of a ride to the Homecoming football game.

To my parents, I am all-American, and the sacrifices they made in leaving Korea—including my mispronounced name—pale in comparison to the opportunities those sacrifices gave me. They do not see that I straddle two cultures, nor that I feel displaced in the only country I know. I identify with Americans, but Americans do not identify with me. I've never known what it's like to belong to a community—neither one at large, nor of an extended family. I know more about Europe than the continent my ancestors unmistakably come from. I sometimes wonder, as I did that day in the dry cleaner's, if I would be a happier person had my parents stayed in Korea.

I first began to consider this thought around the time I decided to go to graduate school. It had been a compromise: my parents wanted me to go to law school; I wanted to skip the starched-collar track and be a writer—the hungrier the better. But after 20-some years of following their wishes and meeting all of their expectations, I couldn't bring myself to disobey or disappoint. A writing career is riskier than law, I remember thinking. If I'm a failure and my life is a washout, then what does that make my parents' lives?

I know that many of my friends had to choose between pleasing their parents and being true to themselves. But for the children of immigrants, the choice seems more complicated, a happy outcome impossible. By making the biggest move of their lives for me, my parents indentured me to the largest debt imaginable—I owe them the fulfillment of their hopes for me.

It tore me up inside to suppress my dream, but I went to a school for a Ph.D. in English literature, thinking I had found the perfect compromise. I would be able to write at least about books while pursuing a graduate degree. Predictably, it didn't work out. How could I labor for five years in a program I had no passion for? When I finally left school, my parents were disappointed, but since it wasn't what they wanted me to do, they weren't devastated. I, on the other hand, felt I was staring at the bottom of the abyss. I had seen the flaw in my life of halfwayness, in my planned life of compromises.

I hadn't thought about my love life, but I had a vague plan to make concessions there, too. Though they raised me as an American, my parents expect me to marry someone Korean and give them grandchildren who look like them. This didn't seem like such a huge request when I was 14, but now I don't know what I'm going to do. I've never been in love with someone I dated, or dated someone I loved. (Since I can't bring myself even to entertain the thought of marrying the non-Korean men I'm attracted to, I've been dating only those I know I can stay clearheaded about.) And as I near that age when the question of marriage stalks every relationship, I can't help but wonder if my parents' expectations are responsible for the lack of passion in my life.

My parents didn't want their daughter to be Korean, but they don't want her fully American, either. Children of immigrants are living paradoxes. We are the first generation and the last. We are in this country for its opportunities, yet filial duty binds us. When my parents boarded the plane, they knew they were embarking on a rough trip. I don't think they imagined the rocks in the path of their daughter who can't even pronounce her own name.

List of Cultures

After reading "The Good Daughter," the next step in getting my students to write about culture/community involves letting them discover just how big that web of culture is. I begin by asking students some of the different groups they see on campus (I ask them to consider what groups eat lunch together). Common responses include Puente, AVID, Latino, white, Asian, cheerleaders, football players (followed by a list of sports), yearbook, JROTC, honors students, and special education students. After that, students start to branch out a bit, bringing in various subcultures like Goths, Emo, surfers, preps, loners, and even teachers.

Students then get into groups of three or four and begin brainstorming subcultures that they see in the neighborhood. While they are brainstorming, I begin putting my list up on the whiteboard to generate further thinking. For some reason, this is always a fun, laughter-filled activity. At some point, I give each group one marker and have them add a list of as many subcultures as they can think of to the list that I have begun. The rest of the class is instructed to add anything on the whiteboard that they do not have on their own sheets.

We briefly discuss what makes a subculture or community—usually, there's a particular way of thinking or behaving that binds members of the subculture/community. Often, there are specific ways that people dress, talk, or act to show that they belong to the subculture/community.

Next, students will identify all the subcultures that they see themselves belonging to. From this list, I ask them to choose about five that they would be interested in working with, and jotting down specific facets of the subculture—fashion, language, behavior, principles/qualities.

I ask volunteers to jot down everything that is up on the whiteboard, which one of my aides will then type; this list will be distributed to the class the next day so everyone has several categories to choose from. I have included the list from last year's class (which includes my list).

SAMPLE COMMUNITIES / SUBCULTURES

Puente	Water polo	Key Club
Latino	Tennis	Friday Night Live
White	Yearbook	Goth
Asian	Special ed	Cutters
Non-English (EL)	Guys who pick up trash	Skateboarders
African-American	Saturday School people	Surfers
Polynesian	Freshmen	Hip-hop
Non-Mexican Latino	Sophomores	Wannabe gangstas
Cheerleaders	Juniors	Teachers
Football	Seniors	Administrators
Baseball	College students	Coaches
Softball	Honors students	Secretaries
Soccer	Science Club	AVID

135

SAMPLE COMMUNITIES / SUBCULTURES (CONT.)

JROTC	McDonald's	Boy Scouts parents
Band	Raiders fans	Church
Choir	Raiders haters	Faculty book club
ASB	Angels fans	Montecilo
Loners	Dodgers fans	Ethnographer
Preps	Believers in lost causes	Stenographer
Library at lunchers	Sports teams	American Studies
Recent immigrants	Environmentalists	English teachers
Parents	Minutemen	Puente teachers
Homeless people	Golfers	Anaheim Puente staff
Professors	Government people	AP instructors
Doctors	Politicians	WASC suckers
Nurses	Terrorists	Homeowners
Police	Unions	Travelers
Fire-fighters	Musicians	Readers
Army	Disney workers	Moderates
Navy	Dancers	Rock climbers
Air Force	Artists	South County residents
Marines	Computer users	Californians
CIA	Texas	Generation X
FBI	Brea	CSUF
Republicans	Joggers	My family
Democrats	Parents	My wife's family
People from the South	Husbands	Bruce Springsteen fans
Rich people	Teachers	Middle-aged people
Poor people	Professors	Scuba divers
Hippies	Little League parents	Pool players
Prisoners	AYSO parents	Church
Gang members	Ice-Skating parents	Angels fans
Weight lifters	Drama parents	Magnolia High School

Reading About Culture

Over the course of the next few days, we will work at describing our communities or subcultures in various ways—I have had students do quick writes, poems, and descriptive pieces before. I will emphasize using imagery and metaphor at this stage. We also read community- or culture-based writing, including the following:

- "Sonrisas" and "Elena" by Pat Mora
- Excerpts from *Becoming Mexican-American* by George Sanchez
- "What Boyfriend Told Me at Age Seventeen" and "JohnwannabeChicano" by Michele Serros
- "What It Means to Be Latino" by Dr. Clara E. Rodriguez
- "At the Crossroads: Latinos in the New Millennium" by Rubén Martinez
- Samples from previous students, including "Comida" by Lorena Camarena

We will approach all these works with a highlighter, spotting imagery, metaphor, and strong lines; we will then discuss in a type of Socratic seminar format and write about how each piece adds to our ongoing examination of culture.

Through Puente, I am lucky to work with some incredible English teachers. Two of them, Kristin Land and Krista Rogerson, at Tennyson High School in Northern California, use the poem "Elena" in a Socratic seminar format. I used their materials this past year and am quite happy with the results. As with "The Good Daughter," I begin by letting the class see the title and anticipate what they will be reading. Then, we read the entire poem twice: I read it out loud once, and then a student reads it out loud.

"Elena"

BY PAT MORA

> My Spanish isn't enough.
> I remember how I'd smile
> listening to my little ones,
> understanding every word they'd say,

137

their jokes, their songs, their plots.
  Vamos a pedirle dulces a mamá. Vamos.
but that was in Mexico.
Now my children go to American high schools.
They speak English. At night they sit around
the kitchen table, laugh with one another.
I stand by the stove and feel dumb, alone.
I bought a book to learn English.
My husband frowned, drank more beer.
My oldest said, "*Mamá,* he doesn't want you
to be smarter than he is." I'm forty,
embarrassed at mispronouncing words,
embarrassed at the laughter of my children,
the grocer, the mailman. Sometimes I take
my English book and lock myself in the bathroom,
say the thick words softly,
for if I stop trying, I will be deaf
when my children need my help.

Socratic Seminar Conversational Moves

A Socratic seminar is a powerful experience for students. Basically put, a Socratic seminar is a lengthy discussion in which students participate with an open mind and a willingness to listen and consider other points of view. The teacher usually remains silent, making notes on who participates and the depth of thinking and analysis in each point of view. It is not a debate in which participants are trying to convince others but a dialogue in which students are trying to understand other students.

In a nutshell, students prepare to engage in an open-ended discussion about a concept or text. They talk without being controlled by the instructor. If there is an audience, they usually take notes on the main points being made, but they do not engage in the discussion.

Land and Rogerson have students first write out what questions or ideas come to mind as students reread the poem. Then, first in pairs and then in groups of four, students share their ideas/questions with each other. During this time, they choose one individual from each group to take part in the Socratic seminar. Students are representing their groups at this point, and the student who is part of the seminar will earn a grade for each person in the group; thus, the group looks at its time discussing the poem as preparation for the conversation.

Further, they provide what they call "conversational moves" to help students articulate their views. Here are the conversational moves of theirs that I have used:

- Ask for clarification of a portion of the text.
- Ask someone to clarify his or her commentary on the text.
- Ask or respond to an interpretive question about the text.
- Add or extend another student's commentary.
- Ask for evidence to support a student's commentary on the text.
- Ask for evidence to support a comment about the text.
- Agree with an idea and explain why.
- Offer an alternative view to an idea.
- Make connections between different parts of the text, between the text and yourself, other texts, or world events.

They also review conduct expectations:

- Come to the discussion prepared.
- Listen and speak respectfully.
- Pay attention carefully.
- Acknowledge the ideas of others.
- Do not dominate the conversation.
- Encourage others to participate.
- Respond respectfully to those with whom you disagree.
- Keep an open mind.
- Take risks.

I always prepare students for Socratic seminar by sharing the importance of keeping the conversation going. It is just like being on a first date—you don't ever say to the other person "I'm done talking now." When we go out with someone for the first time, we ask further questions and offer our views, all in an effort to get to know the other person better. Socratic seminar is just like that.

In order to keep the conversation flowing, Land and Rogerson offer several conversational stems that I have used with success in class:

CLARIFICATION

Ask someone to clarify his ideas or to explain confusing parts of the text.
- Are you saying...?
- What do you mean by...?
- Can you explain what's going on when...?
- I don't understand the part where...

EVIDENCE

Ask someone to show you proof or supply your own.
- What makes you think...?
- Are there other examples to support your point?
- How do you know...?
- The passage _____ illustrates...

ANALYSIS/INTERPRETATION

Ask or answer an open question.
- What could _____ symbolize?
- Why does _____ do _____?
- The comparison of _____ to _____ shows...
- What does the imagery of _____ suggest?
- _____ illustrates _____ because...

AGREE/DISAGREE

Show you were listening and offer new evidence to support an idea.
- I agree with what _____ said because...
- My idea is related to _____'s idea...
- I see it another way because...
- Couldn't you also say...?

After the Socratic seminar is over, I ask my students to write a quick, one-page reflection on what points stood out to them from the discussion. Students who were actually in the discussion are asked to write a quick, one-page reflection on their performance—what they learned, what views were changed, what they held back, etc.

The following day, I will usually do a piece of nonfiction with the students and then return to Socratic seminar again, this time with a student poem written a number of years ago. I follow the same format but choose different students.

"Comida"
BY LORENA CAMARENA

Mi Mami y Papi offer me comida
The hands that serve the food:
Brown worked hands, filled with amor
Beautiful.
The creamy,
Comforting,
Warm,
Mole is brought to me.
Its fun spicy chicken comforts me inside.
I eat … I talk.
This sweet,
Accepting mole,
Protects me.
Loves me.
Pizza is the food of the students.
The hands that serve this food:
Gloved, educated, "successful," hands.
Empty.
The cold pizza is put in front of me.
I take a piece, with puddles of orange
grease on each pepperoni.
And put it in my mouth.
I eat … I study.

141

The undercooked piece is hard to chew.
My jaw is tired from chewing, yet this
demanding, hard, pizza continues to
drain energy out of me.
I swallow the piece
Unsatisfied.
Drained.
This greasy taste stays with me.
I miss my mole's sweet taste,
My heart will always long for
My mole,
Mi familia.

The Community Leadership Conference

Toward the end of May, my Puente students arrive at the school at 7:30 in the morning to get on a school bus and attend a conference at the University of Southern California, organized by Puente. The focus of the day, not surprisingly, is community leadership, and the keynote speaker is Victor Villaseñor, author of *Rain of Gold*. The Puente *familia* of writers is full of energy for the day.

Sitting in the auditorium, I am surrounded by my ninth-grade students. For the next two and a half hours, they will hear a succession of Latino/a speakers ranging from graduating college students to the likes of *Ugly Betty*'s Tony Plana and the author Victor Villaseñor. During Plana's discussion, he encourages kids not to have sex until they have their B.A. My freshmen applaud vigorously, having just examined the data regarding teenage pregnancy as we began the persuasive research paper. Villaseñor follows, exhorting them to repeat, "I am a burro genius! I can do it!" I look over and see Norma shouting with passion, repeating the lines Villaseñor gives them.

At lunch, while playing cards with my freshmen (I lost), Jane Pieri, the director of training for Puente, walks over and we talk for a bit. She is understandably proud of this first Community Leadership Conference. We talk about having just witnessed hundreds of underrepresented students cheering wildly for college graduates, shouting out their commitment to school and community, embracing their various subcultures as a reason to excel—this is what all students need, the type of event that can inspire and propel average kids to pour their hearts and minds into a worthy ambition such as college graduation. We both wonder what would happen if every year, all the school districts in America offered something like this for their ninth-grade students. How many more lives could we transform?

After lunch, the students head off to breakout sessions that they have chosen, some of which include the following:

- Discovering Your Writing "Voice"
- Managing Money While in College
- Running a Puente Club
- Overcoming Ethnic Barriers
- Social Justice
- Yoga and Other Relaxation Techniques
- What Universities Look For in Applicants
- Latina Empowerment
- The Parent's Role (For Parents Only)

The following Monday we are back in the classroom. I ask the students to do a little bit of follow-up writing that explains what they took away from that day. During the sharing of their writing, Susana says that she was inspired by one of the graduating USC students: "I could see myself being her and succeeding." Norma adds that, "like Mr. Villaseñor made a difference . . . it doesn't matter what you go through to achieve, there is no reason not to be successful. Anyone can make a difference in the community, anyone can prove other people wrong."

Alex, who has spoken maybe three times to the entire class, offers up, "I learned that even shy people can make a difference." Mariela, another quiet, constantly smiling student, contributes her favorite phrase from the conference: "Anyone can take anything from you except education." Not surprisingly, in the days that follow, Mariela will be much more focused, because she now has a mission, as do many others inspired by the day's events.

My favorite comment, however, is from the student who said, "When Carlos and Frankie came to lunch wearing their Stanford and Berkeley sweatshirts,

we felt proud of ourselves and hoped that we could continue their success."
That is *familia*, I think to myself.

Beginning the Community Leadership Paper

After we have spent some time with texts like "The Good Daughter," "Elena," "What It Means to Be Latino," and "Comida," and after the Leadership Conference has taken place, we begin the community leadership paper, a creation of the Puente Project.

This concept was developed by Puente teachers and staff over the last several years and is one of the best educational tools I have ever seen. In a nutshell, it asks students to share their experience with a specific culture (which requires some narrative and descriptive writing), then research and explain (which requires discursive writing) how they see themselves becoming a leader in that particular community or subculture. Students are therefore working at weaving together personal connections to their subculture, using a variety of sources and bringing their own voice to the discussion. This paper is powerful because the students are intrinsically connected to their topic that they have chosen and because it is fundamentally about them.

Most topics fall under one of three categories: a career, a social issue, or an aspect of a specific community/subculture. I usually write a paper of my own along with the class, letting them see my paper as it unfolds. I look forward to this part of the year because all the skills that my students have been working on come together in this one paper.

The overall structure of the paper is something like this:

- Engage the reader.
- Explain the community/subculture.
- Explain how you became involved in the community/subculture.
- Discuss the aspects of leadership involved in this community/subculture.
    - » qualities, skills, characteristics
- Discuss your future in this community/subculture.
    - » What is the next step in the process of becoming a leader?
- Conclude in a manner that leaves the reader thinking of the thesis.

The Perils of Salt

Because the concept of community leadership is so multifaceted, I need to get my writers to feel comfortable staking out their own writing focus. To facilitate this, I begin by placing the word *salt* in a circle on the whiteboard. I ask my class to brainstorm what kinds of papers we could write on ordinary table salt. A sample is in Figure 6.1.

Figure 6.1 Brainstorm Web

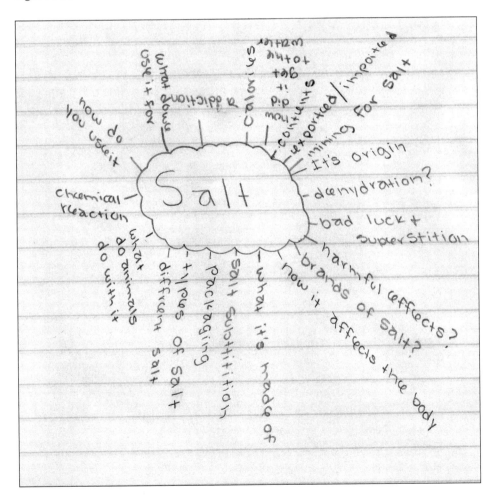

Having brainstormed the many papers that could be written on something as uninspiring as ordinary table salt, I then erase the whiteboard and begin a new brainstorm: community leadership. Students begin brainstorming all the possible papers that could be written on this topic, from specific leaders such as Martin Luther King Jr. and Cesar Chavez to the nature of communities such as cheerleading and band. The paper that I have chosen to write is focused on the world of rock climbing and how one develops into a leader in that community/subculture.

Now, on this particular day, something odd happens. The class gets so carried away with brainstorming on the salt papers that they really want to write on that topic instead. I am confronted with twenty vociferous students, aggressively arguing for the right to write a paper on salt. After the period is over, two students tell me that they are planning to write a book on the history of salt; teaching freshmen certainly has its moments.

Getting Started

This is the only paper that I teach starting with the introduction. I refer to the introduction methods discussed in Chapter Two, and have my students begin by engaging the reader in the chosen community/subculture. Here is the sample of my writing that I give them:

The wind chills my back as I stare down at the hard, rocky ground waiting ninety feet below me. I scrutinize the wall of granite before me, searching for the slightest crack, the smallest bend, the tiniest sliver of a ledge to support my weight, my life. Finding none close enough to reach, I spot one a few feet above me—and lunge toward it hoping for the best. The stones below seem to laugh in anticipation of greeting my body with a crushing catch.

A simple explanation of the thrills involved in rock climbing does not exist. It is neither the physical stamina nor the mental fortitude required for the sport that makes it the ultimate challenge. True, a good rock climber must use his or her strength and intellect at all times; however, there's much more to the sport than just brawn and brain. There is an emotional struggle as well: by conquering the mountain, you conquer fear.

All of these qualities—strength, intellect, lack of fear—combine to make rock climbing an experience to be savored. I was first introduced to it last summer. Surprisingly, the sport came easily to me. Since that first venture into the world of rock climbing, I have continued practicing and honing my abilities by attempting more challenging outdoor climbs while practicing in an indoor rock-climbing gym. In doing so, I have learned a little about the rock-climbing community and what it takes to become a person who stands out in this small but obsessive group.

Once we have read this, the students write their own introductions, often using much of the imagery and language that they employed in their earlier poems and descriptive pieces. After a day of working on this, we share our introductions and then begin the research.

Before discussing the research methods, however, I would like to focus on what the students are feeling at this point. They have chosen a community to which they feel a sense of belonging, and they are summing up their feelings of excitement, belonging, and attraction in a few paragraphs, hoping to engage the reader in that community. There is almost an evangelistic zeal to writing this section of the paper, and it is exciting to watch the kids put their hearts into writing they truly care about.

Many underrepresented students feel that the world of academics overlooks who they are and what they are about—this focus on community turns that around and empowers students to write about their favorite topic: themselves. Any educator who does not believe that teenagers will spend hours writing about themselves should spend a few minutes on MySpace.com to see just how far adolescents will go to articulate who and what they are. This paper merely takes that same drive and uses it in an academic forum.

Here's a sample introduction written by a student, Karla:

As I close my eyes, ready to go to sleep, I imagine how my life would change if I could cure the world, not by using the world's latest technology, but by using old Native American herbal recipes. As I am close to the point of sleep, I imagine myself making sure that I relieve people from the common cold by making them a special tea that will make them feel better. I can just see myself knowing what herbs to use and how to combine them to make sure that their purpose is used to the fullest so that it alleviates the individual effectively. As I begin to toss and turn, I open my eyes and realize that it was all a dream, but a dream that I will hopefully make sure will come true.

I first became interested in the art of curing with herbs when I was introduced to the Native American way of life in my eighth grade American History class. I was very intrigued by their ceremonies, strength, and intelligence. A friend of mine was also intrigued by herbs and their healing powers. Since he had a greater knowledge of the herbs, he then taught me a few ways to manipulate the herbs to work for the good of the people, but it was not until I read a Native American medicine book, did I realize how much knowledge it takes to cure illnesses such as headaches and scrapes. The most fascinating fact I did learn as I read the pages of the book was that the whole point of curing an individual was not to think of them as an ill person to cure, but as a whole human being who needs guidance and help. The person needs to be treated as a physical and spiritual being.

As my interest of Native American medicine increased, I realize what it truly takes to be a leader in the Native American community of herbal healers. To be a true leader, the healer must be intelligent, determined, and committed.

Many of the papers come in following my structure of engaging the reader, providing appropriate context to the community, and then a statement of leadership, which becomes the focus of the research. The advantage to including the leadership angle is that it transcends specific communities because leadership is a quality that, once learned, can be applied just about anywhere. As a student thinks about becoming a leader in one community, doors open in other communities. Obviously, this is an important factor to consider if we are preparing students (who have historically avoided college) for university life where virtually every student needs to be a leader to some degree.

The research stage is always challenging for students because research takes a lot of time. A review of how to do a works cited list and in-text documentation is essential; I also monitor student progress using the same daily progress sheets to ensure they're on track (see Chapter Five). Along with the traditional research tools, I encourage students to interview someone they perceive as being a leader in their community. There are a number of reasons for this, but most important, the interview allows students a formal "excuse" to talk about leadership with someone who is seen as worth following. At my high school, this conversation does not take place naturally—few students ask graduates how to be successful; few freshman soccer players ask varsity players for advice. Teenage culture is too often about ignoring flaws and being unbeatable. To ask for advice runs counter to that culture—unless it is part of an assignment.

Here are some of the interview questions that I give to the students; we also practice the art of follow-up questions:

- How long have you been involved with _____ ?
- How did you get introduced to _____ ?
- What skills or qualities are needed for _____ ?
- Who are some of the leaders in this area?
- What attributes does a leader need in this area?
- What sacrifices need to be made to become a leader in _____ ?
- What is/are the first step(s) to becoming a leader in _____ ?

The interview also allows students to see that not all leaders are on television or are celebrities. Every subculture has true leaders who are otherwise normal, everyday people, a fact that American culture often overlooks. The interview helps cement an idea that the student can become outstanding in a community.

As students research (including the interview), I show them the rest of my rough draft and a few samples from past students. We usually spend a couple of days in class on the research; the rest is done as homework. At this stage, I follow all the same strategies outlined in Chapter Five; I am careful to make sure that during our conferences, I hear their voices in the body of their papers. As mentioned before, students tend to stifle their personality when writing a research paper, so I want to ensure that their commentary conveys their feelings (as mentioned in the last chapter, focusing on verb usage helps accomplish this goal).

During the drafting of the paper, I again become much more of a writing coach for the students. We also score a few samples from past students using the scoring guide (which is based on Puente's standards-based scoring guides) that I have included in Appendix A.

Sample Community Leadership Paper

In the next several pages, I have included a student sample (a finished draft) of the community leadership paper. Of all the papers that my students write in a year, this one is undoubtedly my favorite. Students writing academic papers about subjects for which they have passion—isn't that what every English teacher wants?

THE ART WORLD

BY BRENDA BARAJAS

The Earth, in its constant rotation, stands still as my thoughts race at the awe of its beauty. I am at peace with inspirations dancing around me. Their swirling bodies drifting with the course of the wind. I make sense of a realization that illuminates my soul. I am inspired to create, to make things dance as I see them. Visualizing things becoming their own beings. All this and more is the art community.

Everyone admires beauty, but few are successful in recreating it. In this world, there are many photographs, paintings, and structures. The only force that makes one stand out more than another is the artist. It is the artist's desire to create, manipulation of materials, and his devotion that individualizes each piece of art produced. Yet, the task could not be a harder one for a modern artist. Long gone are the days of Leonardo Da Vinci and Michelangelo when artists could truly devote themselves. Today, society tells us we need to make money to be successful. Unfortunately for artists, that is usually the first thing they have to risk.

I first became interested in art as a child. Before I was a year old, I was already drawing the things that inspired me on papers, napkins, plastic dolls, and more often than not, my own skin. At two years old, my passion was limited to my pet dog and the flowers pictured in my mother's gardening books. As I grew older, I became more interested in studying faces and their expressions and would spend hours daily intrigued with getting someone's face "just right." However, as I became more involved with school and had less free time, my devotion to drawing began to fade. Teachers and Aunts would pay little attention to my art and try to poke at my interest in veterinary medicine, a career they also considered to bring in few monies. By the time I entered high school, it was made obvious to me that successful people make money and by then, the only things I drew were on folders or on the corners of notebook paper during classes. Now in my second year of high school, I long for the days of my childhood when my future was everything I could envision and everything I drew on slips of paper. Had I been less fearful of failing a class, maybe my devotion to art would have been stronger. There are those who risk nothing for art, like I do now, and also those who risk everything in pursuing their love. Horacio Lopez, who received his Masters in Art at U.C. Berkeley, recalls some of the sacrifices he's made for his community:

It's not a real sacrifice: when you like something, it doesn't seem like a sacrifice. In the eyes of others, probably. For me, my sacrifices were more like a "learning experience" . . . . living in my car for a while during graduate school, then living in a studio dodging security guards. Time away from my family was hard, too.

Not only did Lopez give up showers and freedom, he also felt like he held "weight of the world" with the odds against him. "Nobody wants you in art," he said with a tone of sadness in his voice, "[everyone] tries to discourage you."

Another aspiring artist, Cesar Torres, who recently graduated from C.S.U. Long Beach for illustration, remembers that not only was a lot of his "free time" sacrificed for the love of art, but he has also "sacrificed the chance of immediately getting into other professions seen as more lucrative, as medicine, etc." He best explains it as how he would like to study psychology because he likes it so much, but it "requires a devotion of time and effort" that at this time he "would only give to illustration." His devotion is evident in his work which I had the pleasure of viewing during one of his exhibits earlier this year. The attention to detail in every illustration is incredible. Every color used and every scribble drawn seemed vital to the final effect of his artwork. In one piece entitled "Las Posadas," I felt Torres really captured the joy one feels during the Christmas season as well as the warmth of family and friends, which he cleverly incorporated with the glow of candles on children's faces. Moreover, the fact that he doesn't sign any piece to indicate that it is never truly finished was inspiring, as was his devotion to each piece. After touring his artwork, I was inspired again to draw.

However, the moment that I realized that his was a field I would one day like to master was when I spoke to Horacio Lopez regarding the worth of his sacrifices. Over the phone, Lopez described what the sacrifices meant to him:

Oh yeah, it's worth it. You reach a level of understanding only through art, through aesthetics, a perception of beauty. If you think nature, it's all based on aesthetics. Within everything, beauty is in all.

Lopez's utopian vibes may have contributed more to my desire to become a leading artist than his words. Now, the only thing discouraging me is time.

As the times change, so do the leaders and the great art of the moment. Torres has observed that computers that are used as an illustration tool often times replace the handiwork that is his craft. Also, before there was "almost an elite few who were seen as leaders," and now, with a decline in opportunities for artists, it "is becoming harder to become a leader." Lopez has also analyzed the changing role of a leading artist:

Back then, art was part of religion, part of one science. Now, all is reduced to television, to sensationalism. One time, art was to enlighten. It's tougher, it's changed. There's no room, it's harder. And with all the brainwashing.... people don't give time to appreciate art. It's not just a painting on the wall, it's a philosophy.

Artists who are leaders today are different from the leading artists in earlier centuries in many ways. The style is one important difference. Modern art differs from art form other centuries in that modern art is created by "artists who veered away from the traditional concepts and techniques of painting, sculpture, and other fine arts that had been practiced since the Renaissance" (Infoplease.com). The Columbia Electronic Encyclopedia goes on to state that "nearly every phase of mdern art was initially greeted by the public with ridicule, but as the shock wore off, the various movements settled into history, influencing and inspiring new generations of artists." What determines which art will be great at the moment is not so much the artist, but the time.

One artist who is admired today by many is photographer Ansel Adams. In Adams' autobiography, he quotes President Jimmy Carter's words of admiration:

Drawn to the beauty of nature's monuments, he is regarded by environmentalists as a monument himself, and by photographers as a national institution. It is through his foresight and fortitude that so much of America has been saved for future Americans (Adams 348).

In my opinion, what makes Adams stand out is his devotion and skill in capturing Earth's beauty. Every photograph was an inspiration. Some of this most famous photographs are of Yosemite National Park. In *Ansel Adams, An Autobiography,* Adams describes his first trip to Yosemite in a way that truly envelopes his desire to capture the park's beauty:

The splendor of Yosemite burst upon us and it was glorious. Little clouds were gathering in the sky above the granite cliffs, and the mists of Bridal Veil Fall shimmered in the sun. We trailed a drogue of dust as we gathered speed on the level valley floor. One wonder after another descended upon us; I recall not only the colossal but the little things: the grasses and ferns, cool atriums of the forest. The river was mostly quiet and greenish-deep; Sentinel Fall and Yosemite Falls were booming in early summer flood, and many small shining cascades threaded the cliffs. There was light everywhere!

I want to be a leader in the art community because not only is it something I love to do, but a community that we are all somewhat responsible to save. It is important that this community not only continue to grow, but grow with "the enthusiasm for the arts" that artists like Adams share (Torres). In addition, like Lopez, I want to set a good example. A Master's degree doesn't automatically make him a leader, it is his undying devotion and love that will ultimately make him great. I realize, by studying Torres, Lopez, and Adams, that if I want to be a great artist, I will have to sacrifice a lot of my time. I will also have to learn to deal with the frustration of not being able to find a job that pays well and the criticism of others who may not appreciate my work.

The advice Torres gave me was to "step back" and see what I "really want to do." To see if it is something that I can "commit my time and effort to do." He asked me to think about what has led me here, to this community, and maybe even research other communities before deciding. Lopez also warns me that "the role of the artist will change. It will lessen each year as will the opportunities for the artist. There will be a less of a need. Just look at the government: the first thing to go is always the art program."

Nevertheless, if the desire is strong enough, the devotion great enough, and the inspiration undying, I know I will be able to make it as an artist. The best thing about being successful in art is that as long as you like what you're doing, how other people view your work doesn't matter. Looking closer, I think this is true for every field and maybe even every aspect of life: success is defined by the person, and a leader is defined by the people.

Conclusion

As I have said throughout this book, there is no one way to reach underrepresented students—they are as different from one another as any other group of students. However, any good teacher knows that giving students choices regarding their writing assignments improves their motivation and passion.

Good teachers know that getting a class to work together as a family strengthens the focus of the students and increases the time spent on task; also, good teachers know that valuing a student's background improves the sense of worth and sets a person free from the feeling of not belonging to the mainstream that so many underrepresented students feel. All these approaches are beneficial in the instruction of any student; for underrepresented students they are essential. So many more students could be reached if educational institutions and the decision-makers in positions of power allowed students to approach the subcultures they are engaged in with an academic eye. By allowing students to research and write about their heritage or subculture, or communities, we validate who they are and allow them to build off a foundation of strength rather than the perception of a deficit that too many students burden themselves with.

In the past several years, I have watched as the educational tenor of high school has worsened nationwide. In our quest to achieve higher test scores to placate the No Child Left Behind mandates, too many school districts have lost sight of exactly what it is they are to do: prepare the upcoming generation for the rigors of competition that living in the United States in the twenty-first century demands. We need to focus on so much more than minimum skills—especially schools with high numbers of underrepresented students. Our nation's future global success is dependent on underrepresented students becoming equitably represented in the near future. In my experience, the community leadership paper, through the process required to write it, has helped my students to achieve the goal of moving beyond mundane "basic skills" to authentic, worthwhile analysis of the real world; academic research of a valued topic; meaningful composing of collegiate exposition; earnest sharing and responding by adolescents who care about their writing; and most of all, a deeper understanding of themselves.

CHAPTER SEVEN

Reflection: The Key to Growth as a Reader, Writer, and Person

IN THE PREVIOUS SIX CHAPTERS, I HAVE ATTEMPTED TO EXPLAIN THE NEED FOR A MORE EFFECTIVE APPROACH TO PREPARING UNDERREPRESENTED STUDENTS FOR THE RIGOROUS DEMANDS OF READING AND WRITING IN COLLEGE AND THE PRICE OUR SOCIETY WILL PAY IF WE FAIL, AS WELL AS THE COST TO THE LIVES OF THOUSANDS OF GOOD KIDS ENTRUSTED TO OUR CARE. I HAVE EXPLAINED THE NECESSITY OF CREATING COMMUNITY IN THE CLASSROOM, A CONCEPT I REFER TO AS *FAMILIA;* I HAVE THEN TRIED TO ILLUSTRATE WHAT THIS LOOKS LIKE BY REFERRING TO SPECIFIC LESSONS ABOUT WRITING.

All of this is to enable students to achieve their dreams of college through the acquisition of skills in reading and writing. Accompanying the instruction must be a continual stream of reflection on the part of the student (for that matter, any good teacher must engage in reflection as well). This chapter focuses on the role of reflection in my classroom.

In my earlier years as a teacher, I would have students go through the writing process, and then, on the day that the paper was to be handed in, I would ask students to write a short reflection on the process and the product. I am indebted to several other Puentistas, especially Julie Lecense-Switzer and

Mary K. Healy, for making me realize the necessity for frequent reflection, not just at the end of the writing process, but throughout it.

I have included examples of student reflection in the other chapters of this book, but here I will focus on reflection that goes beyond students' writing skills. As a teacher of college-preparatory English, I need to facilitate activities that push my students to reflect on their movement toward perceiving themselves as academic leaders.

This chapter provides examples that I use to get students to gradually start to think of themselves not as high school freshmen and sophomores but as future successful college students.

Field Trips

In my own four years of high school, I never visited a single university. In fact, the first time I stepped foot on a UC campus was as a teacher taking my students on a field trip. I can still remember trying not to show my surprise at how incredibly beautiful the campus was compared to my community college experience. For many underrepresented students, college visits never happen.

Students need to experience college campuses, and those visits need to be made meaningful, with pre-visit and post-visit activities. Here are some activities that I have used both prior to and during a college visit:

- Brainstorm good questions to ask while visiting a campus; create different question "banks" for admissions officers, tour guides, and Magnolia alumni.
- Compare/contrast college visited with another college that the student has visited in the past (ideal for a two-visit day).
- Research the campus prior to visiting—how the reality differs from the images posted on the website.
- List desired attributes of a campus (i.e., weather, setting, size, demographics, particular majors) and "grade" the campus according to how well it matches up to individual preferences.
- Conduct interviews with college students, professors, and Magnolia alumni (or all three).
- Make predictions of what the university will look like, feel like, etc.

After a college visit, it is essential that students reflect on their observations. Simply having them write for ten minutes about what stood out to them helps cement their familiarity with the university and with universities in general. To become comfortable with the idea of attending a four-year university, most students must first become familiar with colleges and the feel of institutions of higher learning. The reflection after a visit helps accomplish just that. Often, if advance arrangements for college speakers are made, those reflections can be quite powerful. As mentioned in the last chapter, this past year my freshmen attended a Puente Leadership Conference at the University of Southern California. Here is what Susana said:

> I think it was really worth going to the field trip. It really made my hopes go up into getting into a four year university. Hearing the students speaking of how her mom worked three jobs just to keep the family happy. That really touched me because my mother is in that same situation and just seeing her succeed makes me realize that I could succeed as well.

By having Susana reflect on her visit, the concept of college success becomes much stronger in her mind. When the class shares their reflections, it can make the difference between a wasted day on a college campus and a deep, meaningful experience that contributes toward a student shifting his or her perception about college.

Negotiations

At the end of January, just before the semester ends, students engage in portfolio negotiations. Rather than assembling an entire portfolio (which we will do at the end of the year), students reflect on how they are doing in reading, writing, and study habits. They consider how they have done in these areas, and they create goals for the upcoming semester. Collecting evidence (reading-check scores, specific essays, attendance, etc.), they then grade themselves in each of these areas, on the following sheet.

MIDYEAR EVIDENCE FOR PORTFOLIO NEGOTIATION

Name_____ Grade requested for negotiation_____

MY REQUESTED GRADE FOR READING, BASED ON THE FOLLOWING:

_____ 1. Number of books I have read outside of class this semester.

_____ 2. Number of perfect scores on reading checks. My reading check scores are (write down your 15 scores):

_____ 3. Number of hours I spent reading outside of class.

_____ 4. On a scale of 1–10, rate your reading. What strategies do you use when you read? (List them below.)

What is/are your reading goal(s) for the upcoming semester?

What books have you read? (Bring Reading Record.) Which one did you like best?

MY REQUESTED GRADE FOR WRITING BASED ON THE FOLLOWING:

_____ 1. Score on birth order paper

_____ 2. Score on Mango Street paper

_____ 3. Score on neighborhood essay

_____ 4. Score on autobiographical paper

Which essay exhibited the best thesis? Be ready to explain your thesis.

What writing techniques have you used? Be ready to show evidence.

Where have you displayed strong editing skills? Be ready to show evidence.

What is one area of writing in which you'd like to improve next semester?

MY REQUESTED GRADE FOR STUDENT SKILLS BASED ON THE FOLLOWING:

_____ 1. Number of days I've been absent.

_____ 2. Number of days I've been tardy.

_____ 3. Grade you'd give yourself for organization (bring notebook).

_____ 4. GPA based on current Progress Report.

_____ 5. Grade you'd give yourself for Puente involvement. Be ready to explain why you deserve this grade.

_____ 6. Grade you deserve for citizenship. Why do you deserve this grade? How could you improve?

_____ 7. Effort grade. Briefly explain why you are receiving this score:

What has been your biggest improvement in study skills?

How could you further improve your study skills?

The last three days of the semester are dedicated to negotiations during which students propose an overall grade based on their reading, writing, and study habits. They support this proposed grade with the evidence accumulated from the semester, which helps them to strengthen their views of themselves as academic successes or identify areas that need improvement.

I should point out here that my role is supportive, not combative. I am not out to whittle my students down or to erode their confidence. There are times when students will inflate their performance, and I will gently point out that their evidence does not allow me to assign them the grade they have requested, but for the most part, students approach this event fairly and afterward seem uplifted by the process. Each negotiation takes about ten minutes, and students write a concurrent essay that covers much of the same material. During the negotiation, they can either promote their consistency with good reading, writing, and study habits OR convey their improvement over the past semester;

either approach helps students shift their perceptions of themselves (and will earn a good score for this activity).

Reflective Letter for Portfolio

At the end of the year, students are asked to compile a portfolio, structured by the Puente statewide office. All four writing styles discussed in this book are included, and I usually try to devote as much of the month of June as possible to revising these pieces. On the last day of school, when many classrooms are bathed in the glow of movies being shown, we compile our portfolios, bind them, and share key passages from our reflective letters, the requirements of which are outlined in the document below.

PUENTE PORTFOLIO: REFLECTION LETTER

Introduction

Lead

Thesis—are you satisfied with how you've developed academically during the first
half of high school?

Body

Section One: Myself, the Reader—comment on your development and future as a
reader. Sample topics might include the following:

1.1   List of books read this year (bulleted list is fine) and next year's goals

1.2   Discuss reading of nonfiction

1.3   List your reading-check scores.

1.4   Focus most of this section on reading strategies that you use—the more
specific you are here, the better your letter will be.

1.5   In what ways do you still need improvement in your reading? How will you
improve?

Section Two: Myself, the Writer—comment on your development and future as a
writer. Sample topics might include the following:

2.1   Discussion of specific writing strategies you've used with references to
specific essays you've written.

2.2   State the grades you received on the three big essays and reflect on why you
      received those grades.

2.3   Include references to how you've improved them for the portfolio.

2.4   In what ways do you still need improvement in your writing? How will you
      improve?

Section Three: Myself, the Student—comment on your study habits and future as a
      student. Sample topics might include the following:

3.1   Discuss specific strategies you use to achieve academic success.

3.2   State the number of absences and tardies you've had this semester.

3.3   List the grades you have in all of your classes.

3.4   Mention organizational skills (how do you keep your notebook?)

3.5   In what ways do you still need improvement in your study habits? How will
      you improve?

Section Four: Myself, the Puentista—comment honestly on your involvement in
      Puente and its influence on you.

4.1   Has Puente lived up to your expectations?

4.2   Have you lived up to your expectations as a Puentista?

4.3   What do you anticipate in the next three years of high school with Puente?

CONCLUSION
Leave the reader focused on your thesis.

As June comes to an end, I am usually just eager to begin summer. Amidst
all the frenetic closing down of shop that takes place as the heat bakes my
portable classroom, I always find a quiet, relaxing, rejuvenating experience in
reading these reflective letters. What a great way to wrap up the school year
and send myself off to summer feeling good about the job accomplished.

The school year has ended as I write this, and in a weird way, I miss my
students. Looking over Ozzy's reflective letter, I am reminded of why I love
my job so much. Ozzy is a kid who absolutely makes a class something special.
He would be the first to state that he did not start out a straight-A student, yet
he has so much optimism and energy and such a great, positive attitude that

161

every day he is present in class is enjoyable. He walks in every day loudly proclaiming, "I love this class!" and squeezes in as much conversation as possible before the bell rings. Yet once class starts, he is on task and has enthusiastically progressed in this manner through the school year. His reflective letter is reprinted below.

Introductory Letter

Finally, the last of the butterflies had died. Although I did not feel the sense of warmth like I would with my family, I felt secure. It was most likely the scholastic surroundings. I had already known people such as my football teammates and Magnolia High School cheerleaders. This certain situation suited me well; besides, what could have been better than starting my freshman year as a football player that knew all the cheerleaders? Yet there was more than just fitting in. I knew that academics were going to take an even bigger role in my four years in high school. Although I am finishing up my freshman year, I have learned so much thanks to Puente and I plan to improve my skills for the next three years.

Section 1: Myself, the Reader

During first year, I have read several books:

- *The House on Mango Street*
- *Night*
- *Animal Farm*
- *Romeo and Juliet*
- *Out of the Dust*
- *Man of War*
- *Artemis Fowl*
- *Chicken Soup for the Teenage Soul*

Since this was my first year in Puente, I have learned so many things that have improved my reading skills in so many ways. For example, in the book *House on Mango Street,* I have learned to pay attention to how characters develop and change over the story or how characters can also dramatically affect the outcome of the climax in a story. Studying characters like this has given me the ability to analyze the character before he changes. This was also the first book where my English teacher, Mr. Turner, taught me how to completely analyze the book. We were taught that there was more than one way to review the information.

There are also several other qualities that I have learned, yet one of the most unique I learned on my own. Throughout all the books I have read on my own, something I picked up was noticing how settings or imagery can help the reader predict what is going to happen. For example, usually when something bad or negative is about to happen, the weather seems to change. Or how gloomy settings have the ability to control how the character acts.

Although I have completed one year in Puente and have tapped into reading a lot more because of it, I feel as though I have barely scratched the surface. I know I do have a long way to go, yet I'm looking forward to learning new ways to understand literature. I'd also like to learn how to understand not only the author's point of view and what he or she is trying to express, but how to understand another reader's own point of view. I know that it will all come in time.

Section 2: Myself, the Writer

I have made so many great positive changes not only as a reader, but as a writer as well. I think that this is my greatest improvement throughout the entire year. I went from an average writer to an above average writer. I have to make my thesis so much stronger but not only making it sound good but actually supporting my thesis through my entire essay. Yet I have also learned to use very descriptive language. One of the most important things I have improved on is my introductions.

So far one of my best introductions I have ever written is this one: "The adrenaline rush was unexplainable. The wind was thrashing faster and faster as I gained more speed. I was paralyzed with emotions running through me. Thinking that I should have told him I wasn't ready. THUMP!!! I had fallen face first into the damp foliage of mother earth." I was really proud of myself, even though it took me a while to complete it. This one piece has been one of my greatest accomplishments for the year.

Throughout the entire year, I have analyzed the fact that there is so much for me to learn. I plan to be very successful and great at what has yet to be taught to me. I think that this program has had a very drastic change in my writing. I can see how much I have improved over this past year. I look back at my baseline essay and I was wondering what the heck was wrong with me. I can now use a more collegiate vocabulary. I have also developed my skill for focusing on theses. I learned how important a thesis really was. I learned that throughout the entire paper, you have to keep bringing up or restating your thesis. I have learned to clearly develop all of my ideas as well.

Section 3: Myself, the Student

As a student, I feel that all I need to do is put more effort into my work. I know that I have the potential to be a 4.0 student. The reason that I'm not in that current range is because I get lazy. This goes for every class. I also need to stay organized and not procrastinate. I know that school is not a challenge for me and that I can accomplish everything.

I can also focus on improving my attendance record in school. I know that next year, I can accomplish a perfect attendance record. I would also like to achieve to have several AP classes. I know it would be a challenge but I look forward to a challenge, just like how I do in football.

I think I have been a good student. Yet I wish I could achieve to be an excellent one, but I know I have to slowly improve. I know that I have the potential to be great.

Section 4: Myself, the Puentista

Since the beginning of the New Year, I have learned what Puente is really about. In the classroom, you really get a sense of family. Everyone is out to help each other improve not only as Puentistas, writers, readers, but as people as well. Being in a warm academic environment seems to help me more. It's not as tense as any other English classroom. In a way, it's easier for me. I also feel more comfortable to ask for help, because my teacher doesn't give me a dumb face when I ask a question. And no one in the classroom feels stupid when they ask a question either.

I plan to use this program to my advantage. I plan to go to a four-year university immediately after high school. I love how this program exposes you to campus life around several colleges. There are also certain expectations in this program. We have to keep our grades up. Our counselor really does care about us. I noticed this when some of the Puentistas didn't have the best of grades and our counselor, Mr. Gonzales, was disappointed. I knew then that I had to step up and continue to get a good GPA.

I know that there is one year left of the Puente English class, yet I plan to be a big part of it in my school. I want to help the new incoming freshmen or share what helped me be successful. I'd also like to know how to do school and I know that being in Puente is going to do just that.

Sophomore Reflective Evaluation

Now that it is summer, I hear from a few of my students via e-mail. Some have gone to various leadership camps, some to summer school to make up missed credits, and some have simply stayed at home every day playing video games. By the time they return, many of them will have lost some of their focus. To start off their sophomore year with purpose, I ask them to reflect on themselves as future college students and to actually evaluate how they are progressing toward their goals.

I've included the form in Figure 7.1, but first I'd like to stress that the purpose here is to get students in touch with how they feel about their strengths as students and to encourage them to focus on a few areas where they might want to improve. There is no punitive language in the evaluation form, and much of it has to do with students' self-perceptions.

Figure 7.1 Sophomore Reflective Evaluation Form

Descriptor	Impressive	Good	Needs Improvement
Attendance—absences	I have missed less than five days per semester last year.	I have missed between 5 and 7 days last year.	I have missed eight or more days last year.
Attendance—punctuality	I have never been late to class.	I have been late a couple of times last year.	I am frequently late to my classes.
Organization—notebook	I have an organized notebook.	I keep all my assignments in a notebook, but it would benefit from better organization.	What notebook?
Staying on task	I stay on task nearly all the time in this class.	I am usually on task, but sometimes get distracted.	I need to focus more on staying on task in this class.
Attitude	My instructors enjoy having me in their classes.	I interact with my instructors in a positive manner.	I need to work harder at getting along or making connections with my instructors.
Homework	I always do my homework and get it turned in on time.	I almost always do my homework and get it turned in on time.	I need to work harder at doing my homework and/or getting it turned in on time.
Grades	I am very happy with my grades.	My grades are OK, nothing to complain about.	My grades are lower than they should be.

Descriptor	Impressive	Good	Needs Improvement
Reading	I am happy with how much I read and am doing a good job of preparing myself for college.	I read an adequate amount every day.	I need to dedicate more time to reading.
Writing	I always take my papers through the writing process.	I usually take my papers through the writing process but sometimes spend less time on revision than I should.	I usually just turn in my first draft (OR) sometimes won't even complete assigned writing.
Writing	I am very satisfied with my abilities as a writer.	I am somewhat satisfied with my abilities as a writer.	I need to focus on improving my abilities as a writer.
Worldview	I read the newspaper at least once a week.	I read the newspaper or watch the news at least once a week.	I do not read the newspaper or watch the news frequently enough.
Goals	I have specific goals that I'd like to meet this upcoming year.	I have general goals that I'd like to meet this upcoming year.	I need to spend some time thinking of goals for this upcoming school year.
Self-perception	I am happy with my academic success.	I am content with my academic success.	I need to focus more on academic success before I am satisfied.
Self-perception	I have no doubt that I will attend a four-year university after high school.	I have some doubt as to whether I will attend a four-year university after high school.	I doubt that I will attend a four-year university after high school.

Strengths: _____

Areas for Improvement: _____

From their lists of strengths and areas for improvement, I ask my students to choose one of each and write about them in a quick write. The sharing that follows is usually fairly deep and meaningful, and it gets us started on our second year together in the right frame of mind.

Departing Letters

It is not enough for me to simply have students become better readers and writers; I want them to become better people, to meet the needs in whatever community they choose. As soon as my students complete their second year with me, when they are preparing to move on—to Advanced Placement or college-preparatory English classes—I ask them to consider those students who will come after them, the next two-year cohort of Puentistas. I give them simple instructions for this assignment: write a letter to next year's students; there's not really much more explanation needed there.

By the end of their second year with me, my students should have acquired a sense of purpose, of meaning behind what we are doing in the classroom. So they write their letters to the new Puentistas, continuing the circle of relationships that exist in a Puente program.

For instance, as my students become juniors, my counselor, Steve Gonzales, will pair up freshmen with juniors as peer partners. The juniors often give advice on essays, working with difficult teachers and/or classes, and general encouragement. It does not always work well; in fact we're probably batting only .500 with our peer partners, but it is something and it does help some students, both the freshmen who receive the benefit of assistance from others and the juniors who begin to see a greater purpose to their educations than just themselves.

One of the first steps to that end is the writing of the departing letter, a sample of which appears below:

Dear Freshman Puentistas,

I want to first tell you to relax and take a deep breath, for you have just entered high school. Further, I want to personally congratulate you for making it into the Puente program. For now, your new goal is to "represent" or in other words, make Puente look good. In order to do that, there are several factors and tips that I have been taught through Puente in order to be successful in high school.

Before I go on, I want to explain Puente's main goal, which is to bridge the gap between high school and college by helping minorities get into four-year universities. For that reason, it must be in you to actually want college in your future and Puente will provide you with the resources. In short, it's in you to never slack, especially in Puente, because it is harder to fall and get back up, rather than never falling at all. To help you do this, though, you must schedule your time and make sure you have the adequate amount of time for all your responsibilities. My suggestion is to apply yourself to everything you do as much as you can, because that is what Puente is all about: breaking boundaries. You must first believe you are capable; it will help you stay on top of your classwork, homework, and extracurricular activities. In my experience, freshman year was great. I kept on top of all my work and applied myself. Yet, midway to sophomore year, I got somewhat deteriorated, because I was sucked into the "Magnolia Bubble" (a term used by a past Puente Alumnus who is now attending UC Berkeley), which holds you captive of its endless twirls and turns. The Magnolia Bubble consists of everything that is peripheral and distances you from your academic life. This could range from outside interventions to your friends. Because I got sucked into this "Magnolia Bubble," I am now having to push until the very end and strain myself for the grade I want, instead of lying back, which could have been a possibility if I would've worked hard all year. Therefore, I want you to stay focused in all your classes, always do work, and never put it off for another time. I understand that everyone has told you that at least once, but it is for a reason because we have all been through it and have learned the consequences of it. Moreover, you should get enthused to do your work, because you get rewarded greatly in the Puente Program. One of the main reasons to do your work is the sophomore trip, where you go up to San Francisco for three days for free and visit universities in the state. Personally, it was a fun and exciting trip to take with your class, because you get closer to them (whether you think you will or not) and you get an insight to the college life in these prestigious universities. Yet, you are only allowed to go if you are passing all your classes.

Apart from the basics such as doing all your work, is getting to know your teachers. Being in Puente means not blending in the background, but rather standing out amongst the crowd. For this, you must always ask questions and get teachers' advice outside of class time. This will help you in various ways. This allows you to have a more personal connection with your teachers, which will ultimately aid you in feeling more comfortable in communicating with them when you need help or personal guidance. With the personal connection, I have noticed teachers will start liking you because they see your willingness to go beyond what is expected of a regular high school student. Moreover, when teachers like you it is more likely that they'll raise your grade if you're borderline, change their schedules in order to help you, and give you extra hints on what will be on the upcoming tests and quizzes, depending on each teacher of course. For me, I have always felt a closer connection with Mr. Turner than any other teacher I have had on the campus. I started my freshman year strong, letting him know my capabilities, eagerness and motivation to learn. He is very willing to get to know you, especially during your freshman year. I didn't come into the class being a natural proficient writer, but as the year progressed I got to know Mr. Turner, I started feeling comfortable enough to start emailing my essays back and forth for feedback, coming after school for help, and coincidentally some of his writing techniques had luckily rubbed off on me. I then soon became one of the top writers in my class, but I don't think it would have happened if I didn't take the initiative to break out of my shell and talk to him. I say, you are bound to get closer and get to know him better than any other teacher, for you will have him for two years so you might as well start early. From knowing him, I have learned that he thrives on students who are able to conquer and strive beyond their struggles and fight to get to the top through all the barriers. You don't have to be a perfect kid or student with him like you would normally with other teachers, be yourself, allow yourself to let him see you struggle, allow yourself to let him see you when you're down, allow yourself to let him know that this won't keep you down. Teachers like Mr. Turner are one in a million, so take advantages of having him for two years, maybe three, because other students aren't as privileged to have such a great teacher.

Puente overall is or will be your *familia*. Your class is your support and Mr. Turner and Mr. Gonzales, another admirable person in my educational career, are your safety net. A weakness of mine was not getting to know my fellow Puentistas, until the sophomore trip, which was a bit too late. I encourage you to go beyond just your friends and get to know others in your class; therefore, this will bring unity and many friendships in the future. For that reason, I suggest you go to every Puente event and encourage others to go with you because this will bring unforgettable memories between you and your classmates for years to come. Moreover, I suggest you become involved in the Puente Program. I recommend that you leave Jr. High in your past, and if you were an underachiever, or just and average student, now is the best time to turn it around and really show yourself what you're made of, because high school is another world and those who are content with being mediocre are stepped on by the most powerful. Take Puente as your guidance, and allow Puente to be part of your life. More specifically, let it be your second *familia*.

Conclusion

On the National Writing Project's website, Carl Nagin suggests that good teachers prompt students to "reflect on significant growth—or lack of it—in specific writing skills," in order to help them to grow as writers. As a teacher, if I care enough about the whole student, then I am compelled to have him or her reflect on writing, but also on reading, on study habits, and on the progression toward achieving the dreams and goals students have for themselves.

With the frenzied pace that many English teachers feel under the weight of covering standards or preparing for the next benchmark exam, reflecting, indeed thinking in general, is too often overlooked. If we truly believe Socrates's oft-quoted proverb that "an unexamined life is not worth living," then we teachers need to instill that mode of thinking in our students by providing frequent, meaningful activities to engage those in our charge in worthwhile reflection.

CHAPTER EIGHT

Puente: The Bigger *Familia*

July has melted into August, and the harsh pressures of the school year have finally faded into the freedom that summer brings; the stresses of teaching have shrunk to mere gossamer strands of reminders that our job is indeed a difficult and challenging one.

I am sitting in the lobby of the Hotel Durant across the street from UC Berkeley on a Sunday afternoon waiting for a shuttle to transport me back to Southern California; I have just concluded an eight-day Puente Summer Institute for new teachers and counselors at which I was lucky enough to be a trainer.

To fully understand the success that my Puente classes have experienced, we need to look at the bigger picture of the organization. I have worked with other educational and college preparatory institutions before, but have never experienced anything quite like Puente training. Just as succeeding with underrepresented students requires a different sort of approach, so does training teachers to work successfully with them.

Unlike most training programs where a presenter leads a group of strangers through a particular teaching technique or set of strategies, the Puente

Summer Institute (PSI) always begins with the introduction of the concept of *familia*. From the first moments of a new Puente teacher's or counselor's training, relationships are emphasized and, just as in the classroom, the assets that each participant brings are valued. The training is planned and implemented by Puente counselors and teachers rather than individuals who are disconnected from the classroom experience. Indeed, this philosophy runs through all of Puente's trainings: teachers and counselors, as professionals, have great awareness of and insight into how to imbue students with the knowledge and skills they need to succeed. Much of the training asks participants to work alongside each other in the spirit of *familia* in order to plan, develop, and problem-solve their way through the school year.

New teachers and counselors enjoy becoming a part of a family of ongoing relationships. The support from the frequent connection with other teachers and counselors, as well as ongoing contact with the Puente State Office, creates a very different dynamic than just being a shill for a textbook company, one who peddles a fifty-pound tome written by dead white guys and then departs without concern for the well-being of the students. Puente values its students, teachers, and counselors as individuals who require individualized approaches to education. This training consists mainly of regional conferences twice a year, a two-day portfolio scoring after each school year, and the Puente Summer Institute, an eight-day introduction to Puente strategies for new teachers and counselors.

Puente Summer Institute

Eight days ago, twenty new Puente teachers and counselors walked into the Seaborg room of the Faculty Club at UC Berkeley, ready to begin the weeklong training that would prepare them to be Puentistas. I quickly fell in love with this group: Maria, who was eager to understand the nuts and bolts of Puente; Trent, entering the room beaming with some sort of internal bliss that either came from a very deep enjoyment of life or an overlong stay at the airport bar; Lorena, who offered a controlled smile, her mind processing and evaluating the program as she walked into the room; Amber, a tall, blonde Dutch beginning teacher who follows the Los Angeles Angels religiously; and thirteen other teachers and counselors. I quickly introduced myself to each of them, and my counseling counterpart for the week, Dr. Claudia Canizales, did the same.

They then met Jane Pieri, who would lead them through a weeklong series of writing experiences. Pieri is, in many ways, the heart of the statewide office, and has her fingers on everyone's pulse. A recent grandmother with a kind, warm smile and a slight Scottish accent that only really pops up when she says *lit-erature*, she has guided Puente for the past several years, sometimes running it almost single-handedly.

Here's the important thing, though: she makes the new teachers and counselors actually write and read. She does with them exactly what Puente wants them to do with their own students, which is probably the core of the Puente training philosophy: that if we truly want our teachers to do a better job of instilling reading and writing skills, then reading and writing—not just talking about it, but actually doing it—should be an essential part of any teacher training. Unfortunately, however, staff development too often requires the true experts—teachers and counselors—to sit and listen to someone not directly involved with students explain the wonders of a particular pedagogical tool or technique.

Throughout the eight days of the Puente Summer Institute (PSI), teachers and counselors developed a sense of *familia,* were introduced to actual Puente alumni and parents of alumni, examined data regarding underrepresented students in the United States, discovered ways to include parents and the community in the education of their students, and most important, engaged in pedagogy that begins with the student and his or her culture(s) through student writing. This approach was summed up by Dr. Claudia Canizales, my cotrainer, as a pedagogy of *cariño:*

> For educators, having an asset-based perspective on what Latino students and their families bring to schools, also allows for the development of other pedagogies which have been proven to foster Latino student academic success . . . One such pedagogy is that of cariño . . . a pedagogy of cariño challenges educators to analyze their perceptions and preconceived notions. [Valenzuela] notes, "a teacher's attitudinal predisposition is essential to caring, for it overtly conveys acceptance and confirmation to the cared-for student." (2007)

173

In a spirit of *cariño,* participants wrote every day, shared their work with the others throughout the institute, and recorded their reflections in learning logs, just as students would do in a Puente classroom. The writing usually began with a piece of literature, such as Sandra Cisneros's "Eleven," or Lydia Cortes's "I Remember," and focused on our own experiences and ideas. In groups, we shared our writing (trainers wrote with participants just as teachers write with students in a Puente classroom), enjoying a nurturing environment in which strong lines were pointed out and questions were asked to prompt further development. In short, we experienced *familia* and that drove us to write better.

By experiencing the power of creating a sense of *familia* and engaging participants in an academic setting with high expectations, participants were able to truly understand how to run a Puente program on their own campus and in their own classroom. One counselor, Rudy, described his understanding of the program this way in his learning log:

> The counselor and English teacher must share the same vision to make sure their students 1) know about college, 2) set high expectations, 3) communicate and mentor using modeling, reflecting, and discussing.

Unlike many training programs in which the best one can hope for is a handful of strategies, PSI left its participants (and trainers) inspired, conscious of a deeper sense of purpose, connected to a professional *familia* with high expectations, and with a handful of strategies. Like students graduating from a Puente program, participants were somewhat emotional at the end, with tears and much hugging taking place at our "graduation," where we shared our writing and reflected on what the week had meant to us. I was overwhelmed at the experience of being surrounded with bright, sharp, competent, and caring teachers and counselors, all of whom were leaving utterly committed to helping the students they serve to achieve their dreams. It was, without a doubt, the best staff development event I have ever participated in—in fact, I cringe when it is referred to as "staff development" because it was so much deeper than that. Raquel Topete, a striking, experienced teacher with great passion for her students, at the end of the institute wrote that the

> ... whole experience has been phenomenal. I've said this before, but really,
> I know that I am blessed for not everyone gets to encounter such inspiring,
> brilliant, and driven individuals all at once. This may sound cheesy, but I have
> attended MANY trainings, summer institutes, professional developments, and
> although I always gain from them, this is the first time that I will leave with a
> total sense of empowerment.

This feeling of empowerment is what separates Puente training from so much of the current training aimed at teachers today. The Puente program honors teachers and values their knowledge, experience, and insight into what fuels underrepresented students with motivation and academic skills. Most teachers get into the profession to actually make a difference in the lives of America's children; instead, under the crushing pressure of No Child Left Behind, teachers are being crammed into cookie-cutter scripted curricula, with no acknowledgment of students' individuality, or the individuality of the instructor for that matter. Rather than developing wisdom in our teachers to more successfully deal with varying shades of adolescent culture, develop family and community ties, engage students in a meaningful and powerful curriculum, and reinforce the daily reflection that great teaching demands, we instead shove down the throats of teachers unrealistic pacing guides, meaningless benchmark exams, and canned lesson plans scripted by textbook publishers far removed from the classrooms. We are too busy "covering the standards" to actually teach students much-needed skills that a twenty-first century workforce requires.

Which, of course, is why Puente's training is so beautiful and so refreshing. Teachers and counselors both leave, as Topete puts it, empowered. The writing that we do at PSI is so central, as it should be in our curriculum, that many writers often process feelings and ideas that hold great meaning to them, much like a Puente classroom.

Portfolio Scoring

Another aspect of Puente's training, separate from PSI, is the portfolio scoring that takes place every summer, once in Northern California and once in

Southern California. This year's portfolio scoring begins with teachers greeting each other with hugs and smiles, eager to hear stories of other schools and how other teachers' summers have been spent. We each bring a sampling of portfolios, randomly selected by the Puente state office, and after about a half-hour of familial interaction, we seat ourselves in a U-shape for easier communication, led by Jane Pieri.

Unlike most scoring sessions, this one begins with the voices of the participants, who have a much greater role than readers for AP or SAT essays. Today, with the hot Southern California sun shining outside a frigid Radisson conference room, teachers voice the concerns that are noted, and in some cases, acted upon throughout the year. These are the burning issues this year:

- More efficient ways of incorporating grammar into revision
- Time for writing and revision
- Time for creative writing
- Student-friendly version of scoring guides
- Language of the standards more apparent in scoring guides
- How to use student-friendly scoring guides in classroom activities
- Is there a place for Jane Shaeffer and Step-Up writing programs?
- Should we keep the baseline essay in the portfolio?
- The need for more exemplars of student writing to use in the classroom
- Where is reading reflected in portfolio and should it be?

The beautiful thing about the beginning of portfolio scoring is that it began with a discussion where the teachers' views were honored, and it demonstrated that we have a hand in the direction of the teaching of writing in Puente. With the proliferation of No Child Left Behind anxiety forcing many educational institutions to squander precious time requiring teachers to "cover the standards" rather than teach essential skills, the views of those most intimately engaged with students are too often ignored.

The next step in the process is to go through the competency chart reprinted in Figure 8.1. This refreshes our understanding of various aspects of writing.

Figure 8.1 Competency Chart

Competency	Description/Definition
Scope	Level of attempt Risk-taking Ambition Difficulty of the task Complexity and quality of the ideas
Sequence	Movement through the text, arrangement Introductions and conclusions Flow of the text (gaps? leaps?) In discursive writing—organization; in narrative writing—chronology; in poetic writing—aesthetic coherence
Development	Amount of support, number of related claims, details, examples, explanations, illustrations, richness Supports the intent of the piece (relevance and significance of detail)
Craft	Voice, style, genre knowledge Word power (precision color) Sentence sense (maturity variety, combining) Paragraph control Special techniques (dialogue, point of view) Narrative strategies (flashback, suspense)
Editing	Mechanics, usage, grammar, idiom, spelling, capitalization, punctuation, indentation, special effects (dialogue), English idiom and word order, subject-verb agreement, pronoun agreement, verb tenses

General description of the scores

Scores	Descriptors
5	Outstanding achievement in this area
4	Impressive strengths in this area
3	Definite strengths here, with room for growth
2	Limited strength—needs additional introduction and practice in this area
1	Serious limitation—needs special sustained attention in this area
8	Not scorable (i.e., too little text to allow judgment)

Remember: You may give the highest or lowest score possible for a single feature without suggesting that this score represents the overall effect of the piece. For instance, a writer may write an ambitious piece, scoring high for Scope and Development, but have trouble sustaining error-free prose for several pages, incorrectly spelling even some common words, failing to mark possessive nouns, or incorrectly punctuating sentences or special effects like dialogue. In this case, the student might earn a low score for editing, though the paper may seem highly successful in other ways.

We read through the scoring guides (see Appendixes A and B) and then read Johanna's autobiographical piece, reprinted in Chapter Four, in order to calibrate ourselves to the standards of the Puente Scoring Guide. I gave Johanna's essay the following scores:

Scope: 4
Sequence: 3
Development: 4
Craft: 4
Editing: 3

After comparing my scores with my group members, Annette and Sully, I felt compelled to change my scores to straight 3s. After each group had ample time to discuss the paper, Pieri asked teachers to indicate their scores, keeping a tally on an overhead for us to see. Much of the room gave her a score of 4, but a small contingent of us gave her a 3. The group, differing on whether we were looking at a high paper or a mid-level paper, entered into a dialogue regarding the paper; some of the comments are presented below:

"When you consider risk and attempt, she definitely belongs in the 4 column."

"The verbiage on the 5 versus 4, what's the difference between mature insight and insight? At what point do we call insight 'mature'? Are we comparing students or are we using the scoring guide to look at what students have done?"

"This could have been titled 'Epiphany Rejected.'"

"The last two paragraphs took it out of the mature category."

"I'm used to looking for things wrong in student papers. This scoring guide is totally opposite from what I'm used to."

"Do you guys read the student's paper and assume that it's a 5 and then deduct as you see them missing some of these things?"

"I like to notice what students do well and then look at the scoring guide and see where it fits based on the student's strengths."

The important thing to note from this experience is that the teachers drive this entire process. A small group of Puente teachers meet in June to create anchor papers (along with Jane Pieri and Greta Vollmer, a writing professor from Sonoma State University), which are then given to teachers at portfolio scoring. Teachers evaluate the anchor papers, score them, and share their scores with one another and with a larger group. Dissenting scores are not squelched but rather considered—every teacher's input is valued. We argue *why* a piece earns particular scores, and in doing so, learn from each other. In Johanna's case, the bulk of the teachers in attendance, and the anchoring group, have agreed that it is basically a 4 paper.

The two-day session ends with teachers brainstorming problems/concerns with scoring this year's portfolios; the input teachers give then sets the agenda for training for the upcoming year—again, the teachers drive the process as well as the product.

Regional Conferences

Twice during the school year, Puente holds conferences in both Northern and Southern California at which teachers gather for two days to focus on a plethora of issues affecting the desire to teach authentic college-preparatory English to underrepresented students. Sample topics have included Pre-Advanced Placement instruction, SAT writing instruction, independent reading programs, community writing, both reading and writing workshops, writer's notebooks, Socratic seminars, revision strategies, teaching grammar, and approaches to generating student reflection.

What separates these regional conferences from some of the other conferences by other educational institutions, however, is that a strong sense of *familia* permeates the discussions during workshops. Also, sessions are facilitated by teachers who are actually in the classroom working with students, and rather than one person talking at a group of teachers about a particular strategy, sessions are more conversational and informal, as if we were indeed a family.

Further, Puente often provides leadership training for those teachers who otherwise would never feel comfortable. In fact, the very first time I ever stood in front of teachers to share pedagogy was at a Puente regional conference. My involvement with the program made me a much better teacher, not just in my Puente class, but also in my Advanced Placement class, my Freshman Writing class at Fullerton College, and the SAT preparation class I teach at Magnolia High School.

When educators are permitted to treat each other like professionals dedicated to a common cause, to examine each other's ideas and experiment with real pedagogy developed and implemented by real teachers, great things happen. On the other hand, when teachers are constrained by test-driven and profit-driven decision-makers, there is less room for real teaching, authentic teaching that will matter years later—teaching that will make a difference in the lives of our students. As our hands are tied from what we teachers want to achieve with our students, the possibility of fulfilling the public's expectation of preparing its sons and daughters for the twenty-first century fades, and the dreams of far too many underrepresented students go unrealized.

Conclusion

What I love most about Puente is that it is authentic. The program has integrity; those at the state office truly care about the students entrusted to all of us, and those of us who teach and counsel match that caring.

Leaving the Puente Summer Institute in Berkeley, six of the participants and I share a shuttle to the airport. Once there, we wait for each other through the check-in process and then again through the long security checkpoint. As a unit, we move up the escalator, feeling the moments of the week slowly drip to an end. I am reminded of the times growing up, when the bus from church camp would slowly pull up to take us back home, and we so desperately wanted to prolong the intense emotion and camaraderie that camp brings. We approach the large screen proclaiming the various gates scattered throughout the airport, our separate departure points looming before us. We stare at the screen. No one wants to leave. Finally, Lorena postpones the goodbyes by suggesting a drink in the airport bar; as one, we all agree.

The unity is palpable. I have never left any other training session feeling so connected to my colleagues. I wonder why all of education cannot work the same way.

The adrenaline rush of the last eight days finally subsides, and I sit and imagine a world where the controllers of the educational purse strings and the decision-makers in our various government agencies actually value teachers and free us to teach with creativity and passion, far from the insane grip of textbook publishers and test prep consultants. I sit there in the crowded terminal, daydreaming that teachers, empowered by school boards and administrations, let the concept of *familia* and a pedagogy of *cariño* filter into their classrooms. With such nurturing of students coupled with universal high expectations, the college-going rates of students everywhere soar, and the future of this generation shines brightly.

Then the boarding agent calls up the first group of passengers, and I slowly make my way to the worn seat toward the back, with the smell of stale air hanging in the plane.

CHAPTER NINE

Conclusion

....

HERE'S A QUESTION FOR YOU: WHICH COUNTRY IS THE RICHEST IN
THE WORLD, HAS THE LARGEST MILITARY, IS THE CENTER OF WORLD
BUSINESS AND FINANCE, HAS THE STRONGEST EDUCATION SYSTEM,
IS THE WORLD'S CENTER OF INNOVATION AND INVENTION, HAS A
CURRENCY THAT IS THE WORLD STANDARD OF VALUE, AND HAS THE
HIGHEST STANDARD OF LIVING?

....

The answer, surprisingly, is England, in 1900. A century later, of course, they
were supplanted by the United States, a younger country filled with raw tal-
ent and seemingly boundless opportunity. Today, the United States has taken
England's place, and countries such as China and India are poised to become
the new dominant powers.

According to a colleague of mine who loves research, 25 percent of the
adolescent population in China with the highest IQs is greater than the total
adolescent population of North America. In India, it is the top 28 percent. These
two countries, in other words, have more honors kids than we have kids.

These two pieces of information suggest to me that our country has an ob-
ligation to do whatever it takes to ensure that its workforce is educated to the
highest extent possible, if we wish to compete with other emerging countries.

As a country, we are failing in that capacity. For a myriad of reasons, the
fastest-growing population in the United States does not have the education

that they need as individuals and that the country needs as a collective society. Consider the following staggering statistics:

OF EVERY 100 WHITE KINDERGARTNERS:
- 93 graduate from high school
- 65 complete at least some college
- 33 obtain at least a bachelor's degree

OF EVERY 100 LATINO KINDERGARTNERS:
- 63 graduate from high school
- 32 complete at least some college
- 11 obtain at least a bachelor's degree

(National Center for Education Statistics 2002)

As our nation grows more diverse, this gap threatens the soundness of our workforce. Compounding our nation's problem is the shortage of math, science, and engineering majors; we are wasting much untapped potential and will be unable to meet the demands of the global competition presented by countries like China and India.

These facts made me wince this past June. Every year at graduation, I am one of the teachers who reads the names of the seniors as they approach the stage to pick up their diplomas. For the most part, it is an inspiring time for me, the last step for many students in whom I have invested so much time. However, there is another side to it, another competing feeling that I encounter. For many of the new graduates, I cannot help but wonder, *What is going to become of them?* Every educator knows the type of student I am referring to: the ones who slide by without causing too much trouble but leave school without the skills necessary for the twenty-first century. Their jobs are disappearing at a time when the United States has need of workers that are highly skilled with lots of technical expertise and a mastery of communication skills.

The question for many of us in education is how best to enable students of all ethnicities to succeed academically. For me, many of the answers came when I began teaching in a program called Puente, aimed at benefiting under-represented students with quality instruction, counseling, and mentoring.

Although it required very little money (simply training existing teachers and counselors and providing some new money for books, field trips, and mentoring activities), this program has made dramatic changes to my high school in Anaheim, California.

By utilizing concepts such as building a community in the classroom—what I refer to as *familia*—and a pedagogy of *cariño,* viewing underrepresented students' home culture as an asset rather than a detractor, and plain good teaching, Magnolia High School has risen from the near bottom of my school district to the near top in many ways. Our Puente college-going rates at Magnolia High School are well over 90 percent every year since 1999, our four-year college-going rates are between 57 and 77 percent each year since 2002 (Puente Project 2006), and 100 percent of my Puente students have passed the California High School Exit Exam in English *on the first try.* The only three students in the forty-plus years of Magnolia High School's existence to earn admission to Stanford University were all Puente students, as was the sole student to earn admission to Harvard University. Our AP classes are no longer populated solely by white and Asian students, and students of all ethnicities are taking the SAT exams now, with nearly 100 percent participation by Puente students.

As a citizen, I see the need for programs like Puente to exist in nearly every high school in America. Simply by diverting the ridiculous amount of money spent on test-preparation consultants and resources, we could make this happen (Bracey 2005). According to "No Child Left Behind: Where Does the Money Go?" by Gerald W. Bracey, Congress approved $20.5 billion for the school year 2005–2006—this is just the federal money being wasted; the states are also spending billions of dollars for test preparation (2005); Puente costs only $1.3 million for thirty-three high schools served.

As a parent, I realize that the future of my own children is intertwined with the success of their overall generation—I shudder to think what will happen if we fail to improve the statistics that currently exist.

As a teacher, I have seen the wonderful benefits of programs like Puente. Seventeen years ago, I became a teacher in order to change lives—Puente has magnified those opportunities. Students who want to go to college, through good instruction, *familia,* and a pedagogy of *cariño,* have seen those dreams come true, and given back to the community and the students following in their wake. Marivel Serrano, a student at Blair International Baccalaureate School, described the program this way:

> To be a puentista means that you are searching for that "bridge" to success. A puentista includes those disadvantaged students that will succeed to prove others wrong . . . I would say that a puentista is like a hiker, hiking the bridge, knocking down all the obstacles in the way to finally reach a goal that he or she has longed for.

This attitude builds from the culture of the classroom that is focused on underrepresented students and spreads outward through the school. Puente has also invested in my own training, providing me with ample opportunity to learn from experts and colleagues in education, and valued the role of the teacher rather than undermining it. In short, it has illustrated for me what education ought to be, what it can be.

As I put these final thoughts down on paper, the summer is drawing to a close and my thoughts turn back to the last year. Little League is long over, with my son's team, the Wildcats, winning his league's championship. The wilting lettuce served in the Teacher's Lounge and broken copy machines are barely memories, replaced by the enjoyment of a daily lunch that lasts longer than twenty-two minutes. In spite of the pleasures of summer, however, I miss my students.

In a few weeks, I'll see them again. Some students have been in touch with me, asking questions about their summer reading assignment of *Rain of Gold* and the paper that is due at the beginning of the school year. Destiny and Norma have inquired about their portfolio results. In spite of the dark statistics, in my little corner of the world, students are transforming from nervous dreamers into academic successes. More important, the techniques we have used at Magnolia High School to generate that success can be replicated elsewhere: involved teachers, tapping into a student's culture to make instruction meaningful, creating a sense of community or *familia,* immersing students in a rigorous reading and writing curriculum, and providing opportunities for meaningful college visits.

185

And most important, a competent and caring counselor is key. The successes that my high school has experienced are largely due to Steve Gonzales, arguably the finest counselor in the business. His compassion and dedication to students is unsurpassed and has inspired me to strive even harder to do all I can for our students. An effective counselor can radically transform the culture of an entire school, as I have witnessed firsthand.

Nearly twenty-five years ago, a friend intervened and helped me get on a path to complete my education. Since becoming a teacher, I have tried to repay that kindness to my students. With a small site budget, focusing on underrepresented students at Magnolia High School has revitalized the school. Through worthwhile training, resulting in authentic instruction, the same effect could take hold in any community in our nation. Indeed, the same effect *needs* to take hold in every community in our nation. I know that there are some who ask if we truly can make a difference in the achievement gaps that currently exist, if our nation's educational challenge can truly be met before we suffer the consequences of an undereducated workforce. I know from firsthand experience of seeing students like Destiny and Norma blossom in a nurturing environment of *familia, cariño,* and sound teaching, the answer to those queries.

Yes, we can.

Appendix A

Scoring Guides for Students

AUTOBIOGRAPHY / BIOGRAPHY: SCORING GUIDE FOR STUDENTS

	EXEMPLARY PERFORMANCE 5	EXCEEDS EXPECTATIONS 4	
SCOPE	» mature insight related using rhetorical strategies » vividly conveys significance of event through details » skillful use of narrative strategies	» shows insight » effectively conveys significance of event through details » thoughtful explanation/storytelling (narrative) strategies	
SEQUENCE	» strong controlling idea » highly enticing opening; closing inspires thought » events logically linked » strong pacing, story builds » strong illustrations with commentary that conveys significance	» controlling idea » interesting opening; thoughtful closing » organized with reflection/analysis » effective pacing, story builds » meaningful details	
DEVELOPMENT	» impressive amount of relevant, significant info » vividly described setting, relevant sensory details » strong characterization » feelings/thoughts richly portrayed; extended reflection » insight fully developed	» much relevant information » specific setting with sensory details » clear characterization » feelings/thoughts described or explained; reflection	
CRAFT	» mature vocabulary; unusual fluency » varied, mature syntax » skillful use of narrative/literary strategies	» strong vocabulary; fluency » varied syntax » narrative strategies used somewhat effectively	
EDITING	» sustained, skilled proofreading of ambitious prose » advanced, skillful use of punctuation » a few advanced errors	» few proofreading slips in ambitious, readable paper » effective, correct use of punctuation » a few errors in ambitious writing	

MEETS EXPECTATIONS 3	ALMOST MEETS EXPECTATIONS 2	DOES NOT MEET EXPECTATIONS 1
» some insight » relates the significance with some detail » states ideas; uses at least one storytelling (narrative) technique	» good start toward insight » relates an event and some significance » purpose mostly clear; basic storytelling (narrative) techniques	» unclear discussion » significance unclear
» clear central idea » adequate opening, some closing » some organization evident » story is easy to follow; story builds somewhat » details usually reinforce meaning	» central idea can be figured out » needing improvement in opening and/or closing » some unnecessary details (or) details that distract from thesis	» confusing discussion » lacks opening and closing » random arrangement of information » difficult to follow story
» sufficient information » main event, time and place clear, some sensory details » adequate characterization (conveyed through actions, appearance, dialogue, thinking, etc.) with sensory details » some feelings/thoughts described / explained	» basic events » some aspects of setting unclear or unnecessary » some details unclear or unnecessary » feeling/thoughts named but not described or explained	» unclear information » needs more details to convey setting, character, significance » list of events without connection to ideas
» standard vocabulary » sentence control with some variety » basic use of some narrative strategies	» basic, oral vocabulary » general (not specific) description » oral style relies on short sentences	» problematic word choice » no descriptions » unclear » tone is too informal for purpose
» generally successful proofreading » generally correct punctuation » some errors in ambitious prose	» more proofreading needed » some punctuations errors » many errors » misspellings of common words	» serious error patterns » lack of successful proofreading makes paper difficult to follow

LITERARY ANALYSIS: SCORING GUIDE FOR STUDENTS

	EXEMPLARY PERFORMANCE 5	EXCEEDS EXPECTATIONS 4	
SCOPE	» insightful understanding of a challenging text » extensive analysis of stylistic devices » addresses complexity of text and possible reader responses	» careful reading and insightful interpretation » analyzes stylistic devices » interpretation covers the essential aspects of the text	
SEQUENCE	» strong focus on thesis » highly enticing opening; closing inspires thought » text organized with points logically linked; » assertions supported by well-selected evidence, followed by citation and commentary	» focus on thesis » introduction is interesting; closing is convincing » text organized with points logically linked » assertions supported by evidence with appropriate citation and explanation	
DEVELOPMENT	» impressive amount of relevant, information that supports thesis » paraphrases are clear, concise, and purposeful » thorough analysis	» sufficient amount of relevant evidence that supports thesis » paraphrases are clear » explanations well-developed to support thesis	
CRAFT	» mature vocabulary; unusual fluency » varied, mature syntax » skillfully integrates evidence/commentary » skillfully uses interpretive language	» strong vocabulary; fluency » varied syntax » integrates evidence/commentary » effectively uses interpretive language	
EDITING	» sustained, skilled proofreading of ambitious prose » advanced, skillful use of punctuation » a few advanced errors	» few proofreading slips in ambitious, readable paper » effective, correct use of punctuation » a few errors in ambitious writing	

MEETS EXPECTATIONS 3	ALMOST MEETS EXPECTATIONS 2	DOES NOT MEET EXPECTATIONS 1
» demonstrates comprehension of both concrete/abstract meanings » some analysis of stylistic devices; some basic discussion of complexity	» demonstrates general, concrete grasp of text; summarizes essential facts » simplistically discusses stylistic devices; may reveal slight misreading	» random summary without revealing significance » misreading/misinterpretation
» clear thesis » adequate opening, some closing » some organization evident » most assertions explained or supported, facts usually fit	» central idea can be figured out » needing improvement in opening and/or closing » some unnecessary details (or) details that distract from thesis » assertions and support may not fit	» confusing discussion » no clear thesis » lacks opening and closing » random arrangement of information » difficult to follow analysis
» uses some relevant evidence to support thesis » paraphrases may be lengthy, but are relevant » explanations generally support thesis	» basic information has some connection to thesis » some assertions made with minimal support » textual evidence with little commentary » vague commentary	» single point with little support (or) » information irrelevant or unconnected to a point » refers to the text without commentary
» standard vocabulary » sentence control with some variety » some integration of evidence/commentary » some use of interpretive language	» basic, oral vocabulary » oral style relies on short sentences » little integration of evidence/commentary » little use of interpretive language within analysis	» language difficulties obscures meaning
» generally successful proofreading » generally correct punctuation » some errors in ambitious prose	» more proofreading needed » some punctuations errors » many errors » misspellings of common words	» serious error patterns » lack of successful proofreading makes paper difficult to follow

PERSUASIVE ARGUMENT : SCORING GUIDE FOR STUDENTS

	EXEMPLARY PERFORMANCE 5	EXCEEDS EXPECTATIONS 4	
SCOPE	» ambitious, complex, challenging subject » argument shows complexity and insight » skillful use of persuasive devices/strategies	» thoughtful treatment of significant, controversial issue » argument shows complexity and thinking » use of persuasive devices	
SEQUENCE	» strong focus on thesis » highly enticing opening; closing inspires thought » text organized with points logically linked; » assertions supported by well-selected evidence, followed by citation and commentary	» focus on thesis » introduction is interesting; closing is convincing » text organized with points logically linked » assertions supported by evidence with appropriate citation and explanation	
DEVELOPMENT	» impressive amount of relevant, information that supports thesis » uses relevant evidence from a variety of appropriate sources » persuasive techniques used skillfully » explanations thoroughly address readers' concerns	» sufficient amount of evidence that supports thesis » uses relevant evidence from appropriate sources » persuasive techniques used effectively » explanations touch on readers' concerns	
CRAFT	» mature vocabulary; unusual fluency » varied, mature syntax » skillfully integrates evidence / commentary » cites sources effectively	» strong vocabulary; fluency » varied syntax » integrates evidence / commentary » cites sources correctly	
EDITING	» sustained, skilled proofreading of ambitious prose » advanced, skillful use of punctuation » a few advanced errors	» few proofreading slips in ambitious, readable paper » effective, correct use of punctuation » a few errors in ambitious writing	

MEETS EXPECTATIONS 3	ALMOST MEETS EXPECTATIONS 2	DOES NOT MEET EXPECTATIONS 1
» clear position on appropriate issue » argument shows some complexity and understanding » uses some persuasive devices	» position is somewhat unclear » issue is too simple » information without analysis or commentary	» unclear purpose (or) significance of issue not established » information without a thesis » few/no assertions
» clear thesis » adequate opening, some closing » some organization evident » most assertions explained or supported, facts usually fit	» central idea can be figured out » needing improvement in opening and/or closing » some unnecessary details (or) details that distract from thesis » assertions and support may not fit	» confusing discussion » no clear thesis » lacks opening and closing » random arrangement of information » difficult to follow argument
» some evidence in support of thesis » uses some relevant evidence from some appropriate sources » persuasive techniques used with some success » explanations show some awareness of readers' concerns	» basic information has some connection to thesis » some assertions made with little or no support » persuasive techniques used, but need further work » facts with little commentary	» single point with little support (or) » information irrelevant or unconnected to a point » facts without commentary
» standard vocabulary » sentence control with some variety » cites sources inconsistently or with some errors	» basic, oral vocabulary » oral style relies on short sentences » few logical connectors or transitions » sources cited incorrectly	» reflects language difficulties » tone is too informal for purpose » sources not cited
» generally successful proofreading » generally correct punctuation » some errors in ambitious prose	» more proofreading needed » some punctuations errors » many errors » misspellings of common words	» serious error patterns » lack of successful proofreading makes paper difficult to follow

COMMUNITY LEADERSHIP PAPER: SCORING GUIDE FOR STUDENTS

	EXEMPLARY PERFORMANCE 5	EXCEEDS EXPECTATIONS 4	
SCOPE	» ambitious, complex, challenging subject » argument shows complexity and insight » skillful use of persuasive devices/strategies	» thoughtful treatment of significant subject » argument shows complexity and thinking » use of persuasive devices	
SEQUENCE	» strong focus on thesis » highly enticing opening; closing inspires thought » text organized with points logically linked; » assertions supported by well-selected evidence, followed by citation and commentary	» focus on thesis » introduction is interesting; closing is convincing » text organized with points logically linked » assertions supported by evidence with appropriate citation and explanation	
DEVELOPMENT	» impressive amount of relevant, information that supports thesis » uses relevant evidence from a variety of appropriate sources » explanations thoroughly address readers' concerns	» sufficient amount of evidence that supports thesis » uses relevant evidence from appropriate sources » explanations touch on readers' concerns	
CRAFT	» mature vocabulary; unusual fluency » varied, mature syntax » skillful use of logical connectors, transitions » skillfully integrates evidence/commentary » cites sources effectively	» strong vocabulary; fluency » varied syntax » use of logical connectors, transitions » integrates evidence/commentary » cites sources correctly	
EDITING	» sustained, skilled proofreading of ambitious prose » advanced, skillful use of punctuation » a few advanced errors	» few proofreading slips in ambitious, readable paper » effective, correct use of punctuation » a few errors in ambitious writing	

MEETS EXPECTATIONS 3	ALMOST MEETS EXPECTATIONS 2	DOES NOT MEET EXPECTATIONS 1
» clear position on appropriate issue » argument shows some complexity and understanding » uses some persuasive devices	» position is somewhat unclear » issue is too simple » information without analysis or commentary	» unclear purpose (or) significance of issue not established » information without a thesis » few/no assertions
» clear thesis » adequate opening, some closing » some organization evident » most assertions explained or supported, facts usually fit	» central idea can be figured out » needs improvement in opening and/or closing » some unnecessary details (or) details that distract from thesis » assertions and support may not fit	» confusing discussion » no clear thesis » lacks opening and closing » random arrangement of information » difficult to follow argument
» some evidence in support of thesis » uses some relevant evidence from some appropriate sources » explanations show some awareness of readers' concerns	» basic information has some connection to thesis » some assertions made with little or no support » facts with little commentary	» single point with little support (or) » information irrelevant or unconnected to a point » facts without commentary
» standard vocabulary » sentence control with some variety » inconsistent use of logical connectors, transitions » cites sources inconsistently or with some errors	» basic, oral vocabulary » oral style relies on short sentences » few logical connectors or transitions » sources cited incorrectly	» reflects language difficulties » tone is too informal for purpose » no logical connectors or transitions » sources not cited
» generally successful proofreading » generally correct punctuation » some errors in ambitious prose	» more proofreading needed » some punctuations errors » many errors » misspellings of common words	» serious error patterns » lack of successful proofreading makes paper difficult to follow

Appendix B

Scoring Guides for Teacher Use

AUTOBIOGRAPHY/BIOGRAPHY: SCORING GUIDE FOR TEACHER USE

	HIGH - 5	HIGH – 4	MID - 3
SCOPE	» Demonstrates mature insight into one's or another person's life experiences, particular events, situations, or conditions effectively using **rhetorical strategies** » Illustrates essential qualities/attitudes of the person (narrator or subject) by drawing connections between specific incidents and **broader themes** » Vividly relates a single significant event or sequence of events in the life of the character, strongly conveys the significance of the events or situation through well-chosen detail » May use exposition (reflective essay format) with perceptive, complex analysis OR skillful use of **narrative/descriptive strategies**, OR a combination of the two	» Demonstrates insight into one's or another person's life experiences, particular events, situations using rhetorical strategies » Conveys qualities of a person (narrator or subject) related to specific incidents or themes » Effectively relates event(s) in the life of the character, communicating the significance of the event(s) or situation(s) through appropriate detail » May use reflective essay format, with thoughtful explanation and commentary, AND/OR narrative/descriptive strategies	» Demonstrates some insight into one or another person's life experiences using some rhetorical strategies » Conveys qualities of a person (narrator or subject) with loose connection between events or a theme » Relates event(s) in the life of the character, making the significance clear with some detail, some explaining » May use essay format, with some explicit statement of ideas and support AND/OR at least one narrative strategy
SEQUENCE	» Strong controlling idea focuses on character, specific event, sequence of related events or a life passage; clear perspective and consistent tone » Unique opening entices; closing inspires thought » Essay: Text organized with central points and events **logically linked** by well-focused reflection and analysis within and between paragraphs AND/OR » Story: Strong pacing of actions with effective use of tenses and time frames to convey shifts in perspective or mood; effectively uses **narrative devices** so that story builds » Assertions supported by well-selected illustrations with interpretive commentary and/or details used strongly to convey significance	» Controlling idea/thesis establishes subject and provides focus for event(s); consistent tone » Introduction invites interest and/or closing is convincing » Essay: Text organized with points linked within and across paragraphs by reflection or analysis of key events AND/OR » Story: Paced and narrated effectively and clearly; narrative devices help events build » Assertions supported by evidence or explanation and/or meaningful details	» Clear central idea with identifiable tone » Opening reveals context and purpos some closure » Essay: Events follow loose plan, implicitly connected, or rigid formul limits ideas AND/OR » Story: Narrative fairly easy to follow, standard chronology; events somewhat build; may use one narrative strategy » Most assertions explained or supported with evidence; facts usua. fit points; details usually convey a purpose
DEVELOPMENT	» Impressive amount of significant information about all important events » Vividly described setting includes specific time periods, places, and relevant concrete sensory details » Strong characterization conveyed through specific actions, gestures, appearance, speech, use of interior monologue » Inner feelings or thoughts richly portrayed using **literary strategies** or extended reflection and analysis » Expressed insights fully developed by examples, explanation, extended metaphor, or analogy	» Much relevant information about main event(s) » Setting includes specific locations with concrete sensory details » Character is clearly conveyed through specific actions, gestures, appearance, speech, or use of interior monologue » Inner feelings or thoughts described or explained using literary strategies or reflection, analysis » Explicit ideas and insights explained and/or illustrated with appropriate details	» Sufficient information to make meaningful inferences » Main event(s) located in time and place with some sensory details » Character conveyed through reporte behavior or sensory details » Some inner feelings or thoughts described or explained » Main idea explained in general terms and/or illustrated with examples

LOW - 2	LOW - 1	FOOTNOTES
» Minimal or overly simplistic insight into one's or another person's life experiences using few rhetorical strategies » Conveys or names qualities of a person (narrator or subject) » Relates an event or describes a situation that can be seen to have some significance » Uses basic or oral storytelling strategies; purpose mostly clear	» Unclear perspective on life experiences, events; no rhetorical strategies » Quality may be unnamed or if named, unrelated to events. No central theme. » Significance of events unclear	» **Rhetorical strategies**: e.g., narration, description, exposition, interior or dramatic monologue, oral history » **Broader theme**: e.g., psychological, social, or philosophical » **Narrative/descriptive strategy**: e.g., relevant dialogue, specific action, time, place, physical details, background, figurative language
» Central idea can be discerned » Text may lack clear opening or closing » Essay: Poor fit between events and points, unplanned text rambles, leaving gaps in ideas AND/OR » Story: Loose list of events, unclear chronology; no narrative strategies » Points and support may not fit; assertions may be repetitive, circular, and/or details irrelevant	» Arrangement confusing; no clear focus » Text lacks both opening and closing » Essay: Focus on one point with no further material to sequence AND/OR » Story: Unplanned text; confusing shifts, random arrangement of information	» **Logically linked**: strong sense of coherence and unity » **Narrative devices**: e.g., flashback, foreshadowing, reversed chronology
» Basic events, open to interpretation » Setting is unclear or brief details scattered, redundant, or irrelevant » Limited and/or irrelevant details about character's appearance, behavior, etc. » Feeling or thoughts named, but not described or explained » Main idea may be expressed but unsupported, or not clearly expressed	» Further information needed to make meaning clear » Details needed to convey scene, location » Details needed to convey character » No reference to inner thoughts or repeated statement of one feeling » List of events without connection to ideas	» **Literary strategies**: e.g., direct quotes, dialogue, interior monologue

AUTOBIOGRAPHY/BIOGRAPHY: SCORING GUIDE FOR TEACHER USE (CONT.)

	HIGH - 5	HIGH - 4	MID - 3
CRAFT	» Unusual fluency with narrative prose, mature vocabulary; **precise language**; strong voice » Vivid and specific sensory details and/or complex analysis skillfully explained » Mature, varied **syntax**; sound rhythm may contribute to quality of prose » Skillful use of **narrative strategies** and/or **figurative language** to convey appropriate tone for occasion and audience	» Fluent narrative prose, strong vocabulary with some precise language; clear voice » Description is specific and/or analytic commentary is clearly focused » Varied syntax contributes to the quality of the prose » Narrative strategies (dialogue, flashback, etc.) and/or figurative language create an effective tone for occasion and audience	» Standard vocabulary; some voice » Description includes some sensory detail; opinions and commentary clear though somewhat vague or general » Sentence control with some variety (e.g., sentence joining or clausal and phrasal modifiers) » Tone is generally appropriate, basic use of some narrative techniques (e.g., fairly realistic dialogue) or figurative language
EDIT	» Sustained, skilled proofreading of ambitious prose » Challenging words spelled correctly » Advanced, skillful use of punctuation (colon, dash, ellipses); may be experimental in poetic writing » A few advanced errors allowed (semi-colon, complex idiom)	» A few production slips in ambitious, readable paper » Spells most challenging words correctly » Effective, correct use of punctuation » A few expected errors in ambitious prose, shows signs of development	» Generally successful proofreading, a few "typos" » Minor error patterns (possessives); most verb endings correct » Generally correct punctuation » Isolated vocabulary errors (prepositions, verb participles); errors expected in ambitious prose

LOW - 2	LOW - 1	FOOTNOTES
» Basic, oral vocabulary » Description is general, not specific; commentary or opinion statements, if present, may be unclear » Oral style relies on short sentences; little variety » Tone is inconsistent; few or cliché narrative strategies/literary devices and/or some informal colloquial language used in analysis	» Problematic word choice, or meaning obscured by language difficulties » No description » Loss of clarity from weak technique » Tone is overly informal for purpose	» **Precise language**: action verbs, appropriate modifiers, active voice, specific actions, movements, gestures, and feelings » **Syntax**: verbals, appositives, adj. clauses, parallel structure, subordination, proper placement of modifiers, clauses, phrases » **Narrative strategies**: realistic dialogue, interior monologue » **Figurative language**: symbols, metaphors, similes
» Number of errors suggests further proofreading needed, or lack of mastery » Misspellings of common words (to, too; their, there) » Some punctuation errors » Many errors of verb/subject agreement, tenses, word order	» Serious error patterns (e.g., few sentence boundaries) » Confusing word order, word choice, idioms	

LITERARY ANALYSIS: SCORING GUIDE FOR TEACHER USE

	HIGH – 5	HIGH - 4	MID - 3
SCOPE	» Demonstrates comprehensive grasp of significant idea(s) in a challenging text with insight and awareness of complexity, ambiguity, nuances » Close Reading: Extensive analysis of the impact of **stylistic device(s)** on tone, mood, and/or theme AND/OR » Whole Text: Skillfully applies tools of literary criticism to analyze specific effects of **textual feature(s)** AND/OR » Effectively analyzes the way in which a work of literature is related to the themes and issues of its historical period or of society » Interpretation applied comprehensively to account for relevant data » Explanations may address hypothetical readers' concerns, counterclaims, possible alternative readings	» Exhibits careful reading and insight in interpreting text » Close Reading or Whole Text: analyzes reader's responses to writer's techniques, either stylistic devices OR textual features AND/OR » Analyzes the way in which a work of literature is related to themes and issues in society/history » Interpretation accounts for essential aspects of the text. » May touch on possible alternative reading(s), ambiguities	» Demonstrates comprehension of both concrete and abstract meanings including at least one idea in the text » Interprets at least one stylistic device OR at least one textual feature; some maturity in analysis, some basic treatment of complexity » Efforts applied to most of the important parts of the text
SEQUENCE	» Strong focus overall, controlling idea, coherent thesis, clear perspective, consistent tone » Unique introduction entices; closing inspires thought; may be aesthetic or formal » Strong organization of whole text, points build and are logically linked » Ideas/arguments logically structured and build within and between paragraphs » Assertions supported by well-selected evidence followed by citation and explicative commentary	» Controlling idea or thesis establishes subject; consistent tone » Introduction invites interest; closing is convincing » Whole text organized with points linked logically and/or chronologically » Ideas/arguments logically structured within and between paragraphs » Assertions supported by evidence or explanation; citations included	» Clear central point with identifiable tone » Opening reveals context/purpose; some closure » Points follow loose plan in whole text, OR rigid formula may limit ideas » Ideas/arguments generally coherent; paragraphs may be loose grouping of ideas » Most assertions explained or supported; facts usually fit
DEVELOPMENT	» Impressive amount of evidence in support of thesis and related claims » Defends/clarifies position using precise/relevant **evidence** primarily from the literary work(s) but may also draw on personal experience and/or **other texts** » Summaries/paraphrases are clear, succinct, and purposeful » Extensive explanations thoroughly analyze the text to further the main point	» Sufficient amount of evidence to support thesis and related claims » Uses precise/relevant evidence from literary text to defend position; may use one other source » Clearly summarizes events, background or context details, or character development to clarify and illustrate points » Explanations well-developed to further main point	» Some evidence in support of thesis and related claims » Uses some relevant evidence from text to defend position » Summarizes relevant background information; summaries may be lengthy » Explanations generally further main point

LOW - 2	LOW - 1	FOOTNOTES
» Demonstrates general, concrete grasp of text and/or summarizes essential facts » Personal response to text simplistically addresses stylistic devices and/or textual features; may reveal minor misreading or failure to see complexity » May not account for some of the important ideas in text	» Refers to random parts of the text or recounts bare-bones plot without revealing significance » Response may be based on misreading or misinterpretation	» **Stylistic devices**: diction, syntax, imagery, sound and rhythm » **Textual features**: theme, characterization, setting, plot or structure, figurative language, allegory, symbolism, irony, voice,
» Central idea can be discerned » May lack clear opening or closing » Unplanned text may ramble, leave gaps » Sequence may be repetitive, circular, or contradictory within and between paragraphs » Points and support may not fit; assertions may not be explained	» Arrangement confusing; no clear focus » Lacks clear opening and closing » Single/limited focus requires no planned arrangement of further material	» **Use of narrative in the literary analysis essay**: The writer may include "nutshell narrative" either first-person experience or episodes in the story to support a point AND/OR use a chronological organization overall to "talk through" a narrative work.
» Basic information has some connection to thesis » Abstract assertions made with minimal concrete support may leave reader confused or unconvinced, OR » Details from the story may be offered with little interpretation or analysis of their "abstract" meanings" » Explanations drift from main point; vague commentary	» Single point about the work with little support » Information is irrelevant or unconnected to a point; no explanations » Explanations irrelevant or limited explanations if any	» **Evidence**: direct quotes of words, phrases, passages, and summaries, paraphrases, or allusions » **Other texts**: e.g., historical sources, expert criticism, related literature

LITERARY ANALYSIS: SCORING GUIDE FOR TEACHER USE (CONT.)

	HIGH – 5	HIGH – 4	MID – 3
CRAFT	» Unusual fluency with explanatory prose, mature vocabulary, precise language; strong voice » Mature/varied **syntax** shows relations between ideas » Skillful use of logical connectors, transitions, qualifiers, concession » May incorporate **interpretive language** seamlessly into analysis » Skillfully integrates **source and support material** with conventional citation » Appropriate tone for audience, purpose, and formality of context	» Fluent explanatory prose, mature vocabulary, precise language; "voice" » Varied syntax, shows relations between ideas » Appropriate use of logical connectors, transitions » May use interpretive language effectively in analysis » Integrates source and support material with appropriate citations, generally consistent use of citations » Tone appropriate for audience and purpose	» Standard vocabulary, some "voice" » Sentence control with some variety (e.g., sentence joining or clausal and phrasal modifiers) » Inconsistent use of logical connectors, transitions » Demonstrates awareness of interpretive language in analysis » Correctly presents quotations or paraphrase of text; may use inconsistent citations » Tone is generally appropriate for level of formality
EDIT	» Sustained, skilled proofreading of ambitious prose » Challenging words spelled correctly » Advanced, skillful use of punctuation (colon, dash, ellipses); may be experimental in poetic writing » A few advanced errors allowed (semi-colon, complex idiom)	» A few production slips in ambitious, readable paper » Spells most challenging words correctly » Effective, correct use of punctuation » A few expected errors in ambitious prose, shows signs of development	» Generally successful proofreading, a few "typos" » Minor error patterns (possessives); most verb endings correct » Generally correct punctuation » Isolated vocabulary errors (prepositions, verb participles); errors expected in ambitious prose

LOW - 2	LOW - 1	FOOTNOTES
» Basic, oral vocabulary » Oral style relies on short sentences; has difficulty expressing complex ideas » More complex ideas hard to read » Little use of interpretive language within analysis » Quotes, if present, may be inaccurate; sources of literary text cited inconsistently, if at all » Tone is inconsistent or overly informal for purpose	» Meaning or purpose obscured by language difficulties	» **Syntax**: verbals, appositives, adj. clauses, parallel structure, subordination, proper placement of modifiers, clauses, phrases » **Interpretive language**: pointing out the stylistic devices and rhetorical devices (metaphoric, juxtaposition) analyzed in literature; or the persuasive techniques if analyzing an argument (concession) » **Source and support material**: in-text citation, use of direct quotations, paraphrasing
» Number of errors suggests further proofreading needed, or lack of mastery » Misspellings of common words (to, too; their, there) » Some punctuation errors » Many errors of verb/subject agreement, tenses, word order	» Serious error patterns (e.g., few sentence boundaries) » Confusing word order, word choice, idioms	

PERSUASIVE ARGUMENT: SCORING GUIDE FOR TEACHER USE

	HIGH - 5	HIGH - 4	MID - 3
SCOPE	» Ambitious treatment of complex or challenging **subject** » Arguments based on accurate, well-synthesized information from **multiple sources** or extended observation » Position taken shows insight into complexity of issues, recommendations acknowledge and/or explain opposing perspectives or realistic difficulties » Appropriate level of formality and skillful use of **persuasive devices** » Explanations skillfully address readers' expectations, concerns, possible misunderstandings, and/or biases	» Thoughtful treatment of significant controversial issue » Accurate, relevant information supports position and is drawn from relevant sources » Position taken shows understanding of complexities or opposing ideas » Appropriate use of facts, logical reasoning, other appeals to audience » Explanations address reader expectations, concerns, possible misunderstandings and/or biases	» Takes a clear position on an appropriate issue » Includes generally accurate relevant information to support position from appropriate source(s) » Indicates some awareness of difficulties or opposing ideas » Assertions linked to analysis, explanation or other persuasive appeals » Explanations demonstrate awareness of reader's expectations, concerns, etc.
SEQUENCE	» Strong focus overall; controlling idea or coherent thesis, clear perspective, consistent tone » Unique introduction entices; closing inspires thought; may be formal or aesthetic » Whole text organized with points logically linked, paragraphs build, all functions of appropriate genre fulfilled » Ideas/arguments logically structured, argument builds within and between paragraphs » Assertions supported by well-selected evidence followed by citation and explicative commentary	» Controlling idea or thesis establishes subject; consistent tone » Introduction invites interest and/or closing is convincing » Whole text organized with points logically linked; each paragraph has clear function in genre » Ideas/arguments logically structured within and between paragraphs » Assertions supported by evidence with appropriate citation and explanation	» Clear central idea with identifiable tone » Opening reveals context/purpose; some closure » Points follow loose plan in whole text; or rigid formula may limit ideas » Arguments generally coherent, not self-contradictory; paragraphs may be loose grouping of ideas » Most assertions explained or supported; facts usually fit
DEVELOPMENT	» Impressive amount of evidence in support of thesis and related claims. » Defends/clarifies position using precise/relevant evidence from a variety of appropriate sources » Summaries of information/positions are adequate, succinct, and purposeful » Persuasive techniques used skillfully and purposefully to further main point » Explanations thoroughly address readers' concerns, counterclaims, biases, expectations	» Sufficient amount of evidence in support of thesis and related claims » Uses precise/relevant evidence from appropriate sources to clarify/defend position » Summarizes appropriate information or positions clearly » Persuasive techniques effectively further main point » Explanations touch on readers' concerns, counterclaims, biases, expectations	» Some evidence in support of thesis and related claims » Uses some relevant evidence from some appropriate sources » Summarizes some information or positions, OR summaries may be lengthy » Persuasive techniques used with some success » Explanations further main point with some awareness of readers' concerns

LOW - 2	LOW - 1	FOOTNOTES
» Position taken needs clarifying, or simplified issue could be addressed with more complexity » Information selected from inappropriate source OR is based solely on personal opinion OR is not relevant » Information may be offered with very little analysis or commentary » Assertions treated as self-evident » Explanations show limited, if any, awareness of reader's expectations, concerns, etc.	» Unclear purpose or significance of issue not established » Information without a point » Commentary without a point » Few or no assertions	» **Subject**: e.g., multiple ideas and perspectives on a question; problem-solution with analysis and recommendation; or a single strong position extensively explored » **Multiple sources**: e.g., Internet, news media, texts, interviews, personal experience, extended observations » **Persuasive devices**: e.g., appeals to fact, reason, emotion, values appropriate for intended audience, purpose
» Central idea can be discerned » May lack clear opening or closing » Unplanned text may ramble, leave gaps » Ideas/arguments may be repetitive, circular or contradictory » Points and support may not fit	» Arrangement confusing; no clear focus » Lacks both opening and closing » Single/limited focus requires no planned arrangement of further material	» **Use of stories in persuasive essays**: though the essay as a whole does not unfold chronologically, the logical structure may include "nutshell narratives" as evidence
» Basic information has some connection to thesis » Some assertions made with minimal or no support, leaves reader with questions » Positions/information may not be summarized » Persuasive techniques irrelevant, ineffective » Facts with little commentary	» Single point with little support OR » Information irrelevant or unconnected to a point » Facts without commentary	» **Sources**: e.g., primary/secondary sources, expert opinions, quotations » **Persuasive techniques**: logic, evidence, appeal to emotion, concession, contrast, causality

PERSUASIVE ARGUMENT: SCORING GUIDE FOR TEACHER USE (CONT.)

	HIGH - 5	HIGH - 4	MID - 3
CRAFT	» Unusual fluency with explanatory prose, mature vocabulary, precise language; strong voice » Mature, varied **syntax** shows relations between ideas » Skillful use of logical connectors, transitions, qualifiers, concession » Skillful use of **rhetorical devices** » Integration: Skillfully integrates **source and support material** with conventional citation » Effective tone for audience, purpose, and formality of context	» Fluent explanatory prose, mature vocabulary, precise language; voice » Varied syntax shows relations between ideas » Use of logical connectors, transitions » Effective use of rhetorical devices » Integrates source and support material with appropriate citations, generally consistent use of citations » Tone appropriate for audience and purpose	» Standard vocabulary, some voice » Sentence control with some variety (e.g., sentence joining, clausal and phrasal modifiers) » Inconsistent use of logical connectors, transitions » Some rhetorical appeal, sense of logical argument » Identifies sources, may cite inconsistently » Generally appropriate level of formality
EDIT	» Sustained, skilled proofreading of ambitious prose » Challenging words spelled correctly » Advanced, skillful use of punctuation (colon, dash, ellipses); may be experimental in poetic writing » A few advanced errors allowed (semi-colon, complex idiom)	» A few production slips in ambitious, readable paper » Spells most challenging words correctly » Effective, correct use of punctuation » A few expected errors in ambitious prose, shows signs of development	» Generally successful proofreading, a few "typos" » Minor error patterns (possessives); most verb endings correct » Generally correct punctuation » Isolated vocabulary errors (prepositions, verb participles); errors expected in ambitious prose

LOW - 2	LOW - 1	FOOTNOTES
» Basic, oral vocabulary » Oral style relies on short sentences; has difficulty expressing complex ideas » Few logical connectors, transitions » Limited, irrelevant rhetorical moves » Sources not named » Tone is inconsistent or overly informal for purpose	» Meaning or purpose obscured by language difficulties	» **Syntax**: verbals, appositives, adj. clauses, parallel structure, subordination, proper placement of modifiers, clauses, phrases » **Rhetorical devices**: appeal to logic, emotion, or ethical belief; anecdotal evidence, case study, or analogy » **Source and support material**: e.g., in-text citation, use of direct quotations, paraphrasing
» Number of errors suggests further proofreading needed, or lack of mastery » Misspellings of common words (to, too; their, there) » Some punctuation errors » Many errors of verb/subject agreement, tenses, word order	» Serious error patterns (e.g., few sentence boundaries) » Confusing word order, word choice, idioms	

COMMUNITY LEADERSHIP PAPER: SCORING GUIDE FOR TEACHERS

	HIGH - 5	HIGH - 4	MID - 3
SCOPE	» Ambitious treatment of complex or challenging **subject**; research question well-defined » **Suitable methods** yield accurate, appropriate, and carefully cited information from **multiple sources** » Ideas/arguments based on extensive, well-synthesized information » Position taken analyzes and evaluates complexities, discrepancies, differing perspectives in sources cited » May use a range of rhetorical devices, genres, media to vividly express significance and flavor of facts cited » Explanations skillfully address readers' expectations, concerns, interests	» Thoughtful treatment of subject; includes several aspects of topic to establish reason for interest » Clear methods yield accurate relevant information with citations from at least two appropriate sources » Ideas/arguments based on well-synthesized information » Position taken shows understanding of complexities, discrepancies, or opposing ideas in sources cited » Appropriate use of rhetorical devices, genres to express significance of facts cited » Explanations address reader expectations, concerns, interests	» Clear position on subject, establishes reason for interest » Includes generally accurate relevant information from at least two sources to support position » Ideas/arguments based on generally relevant information » Indicates some awareness of opposing ideas within sources » Significance of most facts conveyed with some rhetorical appeal
SEQUENCE	» Strong focus overall; controlling idea or coherent thesis, clear perspective, consistent tone » Unique introduction entices; closing inspires thought; may be formal or aesthetic » Whole text organized with points logically linked, paragraphs build, all functions of appropriate genre fulfilled » Ideas/arguments logically structured, argument builds within and between paragraphs » Assertions supported by well-selected evidence followed by citation and explicative commentary	» Controlling idea or thesis establishes subject; consistent tone » Introduction invites interest and/or closing is convincing » Whole text organized with points logically linked, each paragraph has clear function in genre » Ideas/arguments logically structured within and between paragraphs » Assertions supported by evidence with appropriate citation and explanation	» Clear central idea with identifiable tone » Opening reveals context/purpose; some closure » Points follow loose plan in whole text; or rigid formula may limit ideas » Arguments generally coherent, not self-contradictory; paragraphs may be loose grouping of ideas » Most assertions explained or supported; facts usually fit
DEVELOPMENT	» Impressive amount of evidence in support of thesis and related claims. » Defends/clarifies position using precise/ relevant evidence from a variety of appropriate **sources** » Summaries of information/positions are adequate, succinct, and purposeful » May use **persuasive techniques** purposefully to further main point » Explanations thoroughly address readers' concerns, counterclaims, biases, expectations	» Sufficient amount of evidence in support of thesis and related claims » Uses precise/relevant evidence from appropriate sources to clarify/ defend position » Summarizes appropriate information or positions clearly » Persuasive techniques effectively further main point » Explanations touch on readers' concerns, counterclaims, biases, expectations	» Some evidence in support of thesis and related claims » Uses some relevant evidence from some appropriate sources » Summarizes some information or positions, OR summaries may be lengthy » Persuasive techniques used with some success » Explanations further main point with some awareness of readers' concerns

LOW - 2	LOW - 1	FOOTNOTES
» Subject/purpose need clarification, OR simplified subject could be addressed with more complexity » Information selected from only one source OR is based solely on personal opinion OR is not relevant » Limited ideas/arguments presented OR based on irrelevant information » Facts listed without explicit explanations to indicate significance	» Unclear purpose OR significance of issue not established » Insufficient information from any source » Limited sense of overall purpose	» **Subject**: e.g., multiple ideas and perspectives on a question; problem-solution with analysis and recommendation; or a single strong position extensively explored » **Multiple sources**: e.g., Internet, news media, texts, interviews, personal experience, extended observations » **Suitable methods**: includes primary and secondary sources and/or interviews » **Persuasive devices**: e.g., appeals to fact, reason, emotion, values appropriate for intended audience, purpose
» Central idea can be discerned » May lack clear opening or closing » Unplanned text may ramble, leave gaps » Ideas/arguments may be repetitive, circular, or contradictory » Points and support may not fit	» Arrangement confusing; no clear focus » Lacks both opening and closing » Single/limited focus requires no planned arrangement of further material	» **Use of narrative stories in a research essay**: though the essay as a whole does not unfold chronologically, the logical structure may include "nutshell narratives" as evidence
» Basic information has some connection to thesis » Some assertions made with minimal or no support, leaves reader with questions » Positions/information may not be summarized » Persuasive techniques irrelevant, ineffective » Facts with little commentary	» Single point with little support OR » Information irrelevant or unconnected to a point » Facts without commentary	» **Sources**: e.g., primary/secondary sources, expert opinions, quotations » **Persuasive techniques**: logic, evidence, appeal to emotion, concession, contrast, causality

COMMUNITY LEADERSHIP PAPER: SCORING GUIDE FOR TEACHER USE (CONT.)

	HIGH – 5	HIGH – 4	MID – 3
CRAFT	» Unusual fluency with explanatory prose, mature vocabulary, precise language; strong voice » Mature, varied syntax shows relations between ideas » Skillful use of logical connectors, transitions, qualifiers, concession » Skillful use of **rhetorical devices** » Integration: skillfully integrates **source and support material** with conventional citation » Effective tone for audience, purpose, and formality of context	» Fluent explanatory prose, mature vocabulary, precise language; voice » Varied syntax shows relations between ideas » Use of logical connectors, transitions » Effective use of rhetorical devices » Integrates source and support material with appropriate citations, generally consistent use of citations » Tone appropriate for audience and purpose	» Standard vocabulary, some voice » Sentence control with some variety (e.g., sentence joining, clausal and phrasal modifiers) » Inconsistent use of logical connectors, transitions » Some rhetorical appeal, sense of logical argument » Identifies sources, may cite inconsistently » Generally appropriate level of formality
EDIT	» Sustained, skilled proofreading of ambitious prose » Challenging words spelled correctly » Advanced, skillful use of punctuation (colon, dash, ellipses); may be experimental in poetic writing » A few advanced errors allowed (semi-colon, complex idiom)	» A few production slips in ambitious, readable paper » Spells most challenging words correctly » Effective, correct use of punctuation » A few expected errors in ambitious prose, shows signs of development	» Generally successful proofreading, a few "typos" » Minor error patterns (possessives); most verb endings correct » Generally correct punctuation » Isolated vocabulary errors (prepositions, verb participles); errors expected in ambitious prose

LOW - 2	LOW - 1	FOOTNOTES
» Basic, oral vocabulary » Oral style relies on short sentences; has difficulty expressing complex ideas » Few logical connectors, transitions » Limited, irrelevant rhetorical moves » Sources not named » Tone is inconsistent or overly informal for purpose	» Meaning or purpose obscured by language difficulties	» **Syntax**: verbals, appositives, adj. clauses, parallel structure, subordination, proper placement of modifiers, clauses, phrases » **Rhetorical devices**: appeal to logic, emotion, or ethical belief; anecdotal evidence, case study, or analogy » **Source and support material**: e.g., in-text citation, use of direct quotations, paraphrasing
» Number of errors suggests further proofreading needed, or lack of mastery » Misspellings of common words (to, too; their, there) » Some punctuation errors » Many errors of verb/subject agreement, tenses, word order	» Serious error patterns (e.g., few sentence boundaries) » Confusing word order, word choice, idioms	

Appendix C

Handouts

Main Event:

ELEMENTS

S
E
N
S
O
R
Y

D
E
T
A
I
L
S

Thesis:

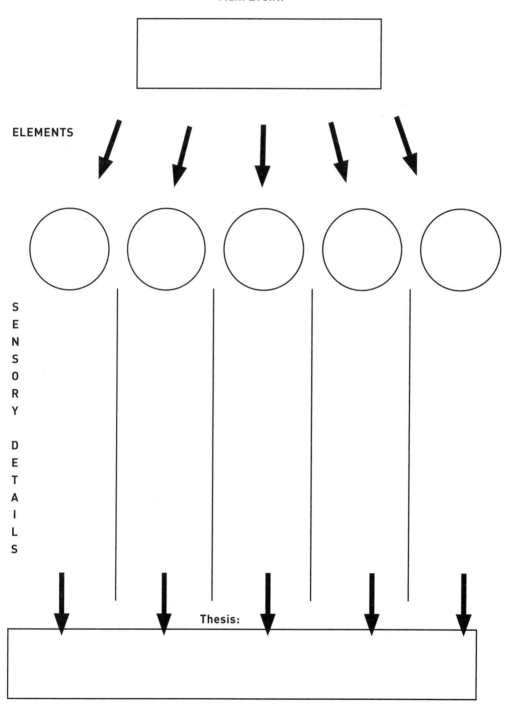

Research Prewriting Form

URL	Researched Information	My Commentary	Documentation Info.

COLLEGE RESEARCH DATA SHEET

1. GENERAL INFORMATION

School name _____ Source used _____

Phone _____ Type of School _____ Semester/Quarter _____

Location _____

2. DEMOGRAPHIC INFORMATION

Student body size/undergrads (# of freshmen)_____

Setting _____ %Women /% Men _____ Students w/ 3.0+ GPA _____

% Students in top 10th of class:_____ Top quarter: _____ Top half: _____

SAT middle 50% of first-year students: Math _____ Reading _____ Writing _____
Ethnic Breakdown (top 5 ethnicities, % of student body):

   1.

   2.

   3.

   4.

   5.

% in fraternities _____ % in sororities _____

3. PROGRAM INFORMATION

Special study options that appeal to you _____

Sports that appeal to you _____

AP policy _____

Majors that appeal to you _____

Activities available _____

4. ADMISSION FACTORS

Summarize what admission factors are considered _____

_____

References

Berliner, David. 1993. "Educational Reform in an Era of Disinformation." *Education Policy Analysis Archives*, 1 (2). February 2. http://epaa.asu.edu/epaa/v1n2.html/.

Blau, Sheridan. 2003. *The Literature Workshop: Teaching Texts and Their Readers.* Portsmouth, NH: Boynton/Cook.

Bowman, Bobbi. 2005. "The Untold Story of America's Future Workforce." Maynard Institute. http://www.maynardije.org/columns/bowman/051109_workforce.

Bracey, Gerald. W. 2005. "No Child Left Behind: Where Does the Money Go?" Tempe, AZ: Education Policy Research Unit, Arizona State University. http://epicpolicy.org/files/EPSL-0506-114-EPRU.pdf.

California Department of Education. "CAHSEE Year 3 Evaluation Report." Available online at http://www.cde.ca.gov/ta/tg/hs/documents/y3ch3.pdf.

California Postsecondary Education Commission. "Custom Data Reports." http://www.cpec.ca.gov/OnLineData/OnLineData.asp.

California Postsecondary Education Commission. 2005. "University Eligibility as a Percentage of All High School Students." March. http://www.cpec.ca.gov/FactSheets/FactSheet2005/FS05-04.pdf.

Canizales, Claudia. 2007. p. 10. Puente Summer Institute training presentation. Berkeley, CA.

Cashmore, Pete. 2006. "MySpace Hits 100 Million Accounts." *Mashable Social Networking News.* http://mashable.com/2006/08/09/myspace-hits-100-million-accounts/.

Department of Health and Human Services, Centers for Disease Control and Prevention. "School Associated Violent Deaths." http://www.cdc.gov/ncipc/sch-shooting.htm.

Duffy, H. 2002. "Generating New Possibilities: The Role of Ritual, Routine, and Language in Reconceptualizing Teaching and Learning for Puente Teachers and Students." Paper presented for American Educational Research Association Conference.

Farrell, Elizabeth F. 2006. "More Students Take Advanced Placement Tests but Scores Drop Slightly, Report Says." *The Chronicle of Higher Education.* February 17.

Gallagher, Kelly. 2003. *Reading Reasons: Motivational Mini-Lessons for Middle and High School.* Portland, ME: Stenhouse.

———. 2004. *Deeper Reading: Comprehending Challenging Texts, 4–12.* Portland, ME: Stenhouse.

———. 2006. T*eaching Adolescent Writers.* Portland, ME: Stenhouse.

Geertz, Clifford. 1973. *The Interpretation of Cultures.* New York: HarperCollins.

Howe, Neil, and William Strauss. 2000. *Millennials Rising: The Next Great Generation.* New York: Vintage.

Lin-Eftekhar, Judy, and Karen Mack. 2003. "Close Review Is Key to Admissions." *UCLA Today*. http://www.today.ucla. edu/2003/031007closeup_review. html.

Magnolia High School WASC Accreditation Committee. 2006. "Magnolia High School WASC Self-Study Report." Magnolia High School: Anaheim, CA.

Males, Mike. 2000. *Kids and Guns.* Monroe, ME: Common Courage Press.

National Center for Education Statistics. 2002. "The Condition of Education." http://nces.ed.gov/ pubs2002/2002025.pdf.

National Education Association. 2001. "Student Achievement in California, 1990–2000." Prepared by Los Angeles County Alliance for Student Achievement. NEA Research, Estimates Database.

Nieto, Sonia. 2007. *Affirming Diversity: The Sociopolitical Context of Multicultural Education.* Boston, MA: Allyn and Bacon.

Pradl, G. M. 2002. "Linking Instructional Intervention and Professional Development: Using the Ideas Behind Puente High School English to Inform Educational Policy." *Educational Policy* 16:522–546.

President's Advisory Commission on Educational Excellence for Hispanic Americans. 1996. "Our Nation on the Fault Line: Hispanic Education." http://www.ed.gov/pubs/FaultLine.

Puente Project 1. "Mission." http://www. puente.net.

Puente Project 2. "UC Educational Outreach—Research and Evaluation, Puente Project." From Puente Project training document.

Puente Project. 2006. "National Student Clearinghouse, Puente Project." Internal report for Magnolia High School. Oakland, CA: Puente Project.

Puente Project. 2007. "SAPEP Planning and Analysis, Puente Project Research and Assessment." Oakland, CA: Puente Project.

Ritchart, Ron. 2004. *Intellectual Character: What It Is, Why It Matters, and How to Get It.* San Francisco, CA: Wiley.

Schiraldi, Vincent. 1999. "Juvenile Crime Is Decreasing—It's Media Coverage That's Soaring." *Los Angeles Times*. November 22.

Starr, Mark. 2007. "Coach, Teacher, Believer." *Newsweek*, July 16.

Sykes, Charles J. 1996. *Dumbing Down Our Kids: Why American Children Feel Good About Themselves But Can't Read, Write, or Add*. New York: St. Martin's Griffin.

U.S. Census Bureau. Population Estimates. http://census.gov/popest/estimates/php.

——. 2000a. "Hispanic or Latino Origin." http://www.census.gov/population/cen2000/atlas/censr01-111.pdf.

——. 2000b. "Diversity." http://www.census.gov/population/cen2000/atlas/censr01-104.pdf.

——. 2003. "Educational Attainment: 2000." http://www.census.gov/prod/2003pubs/c2kbr-24.pdf.

——. 2004. "U.S. Interim Projections by Age, Sex, Race, and Hispanic Origin." http://www.census.gov/ipc/www/usinterimproj.

——. 2006. "Income, Poverty, and Health Insurance Coverage in the United States: 2006." http://www.census.gov/prod/2007pubs/p60-233.pdf.

U.S. Senate. 2002. "Keeping the Promise: Hispanic Education and America's Future. Report by the U.S. Senate Health, Education, Labor, and Pensions Committee; the Congressional Hispanic Caucus; and the U.S. Senate Democratic Hispanic Task Force.

United States Bureau of Justice Statistics. "Crime and Victims Statistics." http://www.ojp.usdoj.gov/bjs/cvict.htm.

United States Bureau of Justice Statistics. "Key Crime and Justice Stats at a Glance." http://www.ojp.usdoj.gov/bjs/glance.htm#Crime.

Ventura, Stephanie J., Joyce C. Abma, William D. Mosher, and Stanley K. Henshaw. 2002. "Recent Trends in Teenage Pregnancy in the United States, 1990–2000." National Center for Health Statistics. U.S. Department of Health and Human Services. http://www.cdc.gov/nchs/products/pubs/pubd/hestats/teenpreg1990-2002/teenpreg1990-2002.htm.

Weiss, Kenneth. 2000. "NYU Earns Respect by Buying It." *Los Angeles Times*, March 22. Reprinted at *NYU Today*. www.nyu.edu/nyutoday/LATimes.pdf.

Zernike, Kate. 2006. "Use of Contraception Drops, Slowing Decline of Abortion Rate." *The New York Times*. May 5.

Index